CW00321924

Introduction

Food Finder

Our choice:

INTRODUCTION

Time for Food guides are designed to help you find interesting and enjoyable places to eat in the world's main tourist destinations. Each guide divides the destination into eight areas. Each area has a map, followed by a selection of the restaurants, cafés, bars, pubs and food markets in that area. The aim is to cover the whole spectrum of food establishments, from gourmet temples to humble cafés, plus good food shops or delicatessens where you can buy picnic ingredients or food to cook yourself.

If you are looking for a particular restaurant, regardless of its location, or a particular type of cuisine, you can turn to the Food Finder, starting on page 4. This lists all the establishments reviewed in this guide by name (in alphabetical order) and then by cuisine type.

PRICES

Unlike some guides, we have not wasted space telling you how bad a restaurant is – bad or poor-value restaurants simply do not make it into the guide. Many other guides ask restaurants to pay for their entries, or expect the restaurant to advertise in return for a listing. We do neither of these things: the restaurants and cafés featured here simply represent a selection of places that the authors have sampled and enjoyed.

If there is one consistent criterion for inclusion in the guide, it is good value. Good value does not, of course,

▲ Creelers

mean cheap necessarily. Food lovers know the difference between a restaurant where the high prices are fully justified by the quality of the ingredients and the excellence of the cooking and presentation of the food, and meretricious establishments where high prices are merely the result of pretentious attitudes.

Some of the restaurants featured here are undeniably expensive if you consume caviar and champagne, but even haute cuisine establishments offer set-price menus (especially at lunchtime) allowing budget diners to enjoy dishes created by top chefs and every bit as good as those on the regular menu. At the same time, some of the eating places listed here might not make it into more conventional food guides, because they are relatively humble cafés or takeaways. Some are deliberately oriented towards tourists, but there is nothing wrong in that: what some guides dismiss as 'tourist traps' may be deservedly popular for providing choice and good value.

FEEDBACK

You may or may not agree with the author's choice – in either case we would like to know about your experiences. Any feedback you give us and any recommendations you make will be followed up, so that you can look forward to seeing your restaurant suggestions in print in the next edition.

Feedback forms have been included at the back of the book and you can e-mail us with comments by writing to: *timeforfood@thomascook.com*. No food guide can keep pace with the changing restaurant scene, as chefs move on, establishments open or close, and menus, opening hours or credit card details change. Let us know what you like or do not like about the restaurants featured here. Tell us if you discover shops, pubs, cafés, bars, restaurants or markets that

you think should go in the guide. Let us know if you discover changes – say to telephone numbers or opening times.

Symbols used in this guide

VISA	Visa accepted
Diners Club	Diners Club accepted
MasterCard	MasterCard accepted
🍴	Restaurant
🍷	Bar, café or pub
🧺	Shop, market or picnic site
∅	Telephone
Ⓡ	Transport
②	Numbered red circles relate to the maps at the start of the section

The price indications used in this guide have the following meanings:

❶	budget level
❶❶	typical/average for the destination
❶❶❶	up-market

FOOD FINDER

The Royal Mile

At the very tourist heart of the city this ancient thoroughfare is one of Europe's most picturesque streets. Crammed around its medieval cobbles you will find an array of fine restaurants nestling between the tourist traps, with more good places to eat tucked down the atmospheric side streets that break off the main tourist throng.

THE ROYAL MILE
Restaurants

Bonars ❶

56–58 St Mary's St

⊘ 0131 556 5888

🚌 Bus 5, 7, 14, 14B

Open: daily, 1200–1400, 1700–late

Reservations recommended

VISA American Express

Scottish

💷💷

Not quite the same quality of dining experience as that formerly offered by L'Auberge on the same site, but still a worthy option. Full-blooded menu that combines the best of Scotland and France in a restaurant that bills itself as a 'happy Franco-Scottish marriage of skill and resources'.

Creelers ❷

3 Hunter Sq.

⊘ 0131 220 4447

🚌 Bus 5, 7, 14, 14B

Open: Mon–Thu 1200–1430, 1730–2230, Fri–Sat 1200–1430, 1730–2300, Sun 1730–2230

Reservations recommended

All credit cards accepted

Seafood

💷💷

The original Creelers is still going strong on the Isle of Arran, as is this addition, tucked just off the Royal Mile. Popping in here you will be rewarded with some of the best seafood in Edinburgh outside Leith. There are two rooms with a bistro-type effort at the front and a more formal restaurant at the rear, though the quality is evident wherever you choose to dine. They

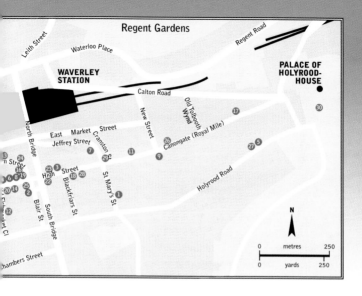

also do their own *bouil-labaisse*.

Dubh Prais ③

123B High St

☎ 0131 557 5732

🚍 Bus 5, 7, 14, 14B

Open: Tue–Sat 1200–1400,
1830– 2230, closed Sun–
Mon

Reservations essential

💳 💳 American Express

Scottish

£ £

Blink and you will miss
the tiny entrance. It is
well worth making the
effort of finding it,
though, so that you
can delve inside and
enjoy the fine Scottish
cuisine that is served up
in very intimate

surroundings – there are only nine tables. Excellent game is a speciality.

Filling Station

235 High St

✆ 0131 226 2488

🚌 Bus 5, 7, 14, 14B

Open: Mon–Thu 1200–2330, Fri–Sat 1200–2330, Sun 1200–2230

All credit cards accepted

American

Cheesy Americana bric-à-brac adorns the walls with a flash of neon splashed in for good measure. It doesn't really feel particularly American, or Scottish for that matter, but if it is a sturdy, unfussy lunch you are looking for, bang in the centre of the Royal Mile, you can't go wrong. The all-you-can-eat midweek lunch buffets are legendary amongst Edinburgh's student community.

Flints Restaurant

Holyrood Hotel, Holyrood Rd

✆ 0131 550 4500

🚌 Bus 24, 25, 25A

Open: Mon–Sat 1230–1400, 1700–2200, Sun 1230–1430, 1900–2145

Reservations recommended

All credit cards accepted

Scottish

This is a hotel restaurant that defies all of the old reservations about hotel eateries. Its

menu includes a number of traditional Scottish dishes (for example, Cullen Skink and wild duck) as well as some more interesting elements such as vegetable sausages and sautéed veal sweetbreads. The steaks are excellent – the Châteaubriand of Aberdeen Angus is particularly impressive.

Gordon's Trattoria

231 High St

✆ 0131 225 7992

🚌 Bus 23, 40, 41, 41A

Open: daily, 1200–2400, Fri–Sat 1200–0300

Reservations recommended

American Express

Italian

Walking into Gordon's feels as though you have just touched down in Italy, with hearty Italian food cooked in front of you. The smells are as sensational as the flavours in one of Edinburgh's finest Italian restaurants, which is an apparent favourite of the politicians up the road at the Scottish Parliament. Dine at the tables outside on warmer days and you could be in Florence, well almost.

Igg's

15 Jeffrey St

✆ 0131 557 8184

🚌 Bus 23, 40, 41, 41A

Open: Mon–Sat 1200–1430, 1800–2230, closed Sun

Reservations recommended

All credit cards accepted

Mediterranean/Scottish

Unusual crossover restaurant that offers a *tapas* menu at lunchtime and a full menu in the evening. Organic meat, game and fresh Scottish seafood are more traditional highlights on the dinner menu. Attracts a varied clientele to its smart surrounds.

Jacksons

209 High St

✆ 0131 225 1793

🚌 Bus 23, 40, 41, 41A

Open: Sun–Thu 1200–1430, 1800–2230, Fri–Sat 1200–1430, 1800–2245

Reservations essential

All credit cards accepted

Scottish

Tourists flock here for that quintessential Scottish eating experience. Explore Scotland's well-stocked larder with a starter of haggis timbale, 'neeps and tatties', before moving on to a succulent Aberdeen Angus steak. Choose to dine in the bar area or the more comfortable upstairs space.

Pancho Villa's

240 Canongate

✆ 0131 557 4416

🚌 Bus 24

Open: Mon–Thu 1200–1430, 1800–2200, Fri–Sat 1200–2230, Sun 1800–2200

Reservations recommended

American Express

Mexican

€

A decade old and still one of the city's best Mexican restaurants. No-frills décor and less than polished service, leaving the emphasis on the food and fortunately they deliver on the plate. Gets very lively with party crowds at weekends, but the quality of the food remains unchanged.

Polo Fusion ⑩

503 The Lawnmarket

☎ 0131 622 7722

🚌 Bus 23, 40, 41, 41A

Open: daily, 1200–1400, 1800–2200

Reservations essential

All credit cards accepted

Fusion

€€

An intimate venue whose walls act as an art gallery, laden with avant-garde Scottish artworks. The owners do not agree with the term 'fusion', but their culinary take on this trend is excellent with Scottish raw materials and the Pacific Rim meeting on the Royal Mile. The dish that stands out is the excellent beef satay with

Thai red curry sauce, although there are constant interesting innovations which spice up the menu.

Reform Club ⓫

267 Canongate

✆ 0131 558 9992

🚌 Bus 24, 25, 25A

Open: daily, 1200–1400, 1830–2200

Reservations recommended

All credit cards accepted

Scottish

❶❷

Exuding a pre-war elegance and sense of calm, this classy restaurant is a real treat in the tourist-packed Canongate. Expect all of the usual Scottish staples, served up in contemporary style. Don't plan on a quick stop as a meal here takes time and you will want to linger.

Le Sept ⓬

7 Old Fishmarket Close

✆ 0131 225 5428

🚌 Bus 23, 40, 41, 41A

Open: Mon–Thu 1200–1415, 1800–2230, Fri 1200–2330, Sat 1200–2400, Sun 1230–2200

Reservations recommended

All credit cards accepted

French

❶❷

Tucked down a cosy cobbled lane, this perfect little French restaurant is steeped in atmosphere. The menu changes daily, though the staple of crêpes is consistently popular. In summer you can laze outside on the terrace or delve deep into the bowels of the restaurant to dine Parisian Left Bank-style by candlelight.

Viva Mexico ⓭

41 Cockburn St

✆ 0131 226 5145

🚌 Bus 5, 7, 14, 14B

Open: Mon–Sat 1200–1430, 1830–2230, Sun 1830–2200

Reservations recommended

💳 American Express

Mexican

❶❷

Has recently been voted the best Mexican restaurant in Scotland and is always reliable for a good Mexican meal. The usual range of tacos and *fajitas* form the core of the menu, but there are also some more unusual selections. Try to book the window table downstairs that offers impressive views out across the city skyline.

Wee Windaes ⓮

144 High St

✆ 0131 225 5144

🚌 Bus 23, 40, 41, 41A

Open: daily 1200–1430, 1800–2230

Reservations recommended

💳 American Express

Scottish

❶❷

Great people-watching spot as you peer down on the Royal Mile crowds from this atmospheric traditional Scottish restaurant. The standouts on an overflowing menu are the red meats, though the seafood is also highly recommended. Décor on the tacky side, but the food makes up for it.

Witchery at the Castle ⓯

Castlehill

✆ 0131 225 5613

🚌 Bus 23, 40, 41, 41A

Open: daily, 1200–1600, 1730–2330

Reservations essential

All credit cards accepted

Scottish

❶❷❸

One of the city's top restaurants since it opened 20 years ago and still going strong. The atmosphere is very intimate. Choose from the very gothic Witchery restaurant itself or the newer Secret Garden, which is the place in town for a romantic dinner. Incurable romantics may want to spend the night in one of their two unique suites upstairs, an unforgettable experience for a special anniversary.

THE ROYAL MILE
Bars, cafés and pubs

The Baked Potato Shop 16

56 Cockburn St

🚌 Bus 5, 7, 14, 14B

Open: daily, 0900–1700

One of the cheapest options at the heart of tourist Edinburgh. Offers takeaway potatoes with a multitude of fillings, as well as homemade soup. It also has a tiny table for two if you want to sit down.

Clarinda's Tearooms 17

69 Canongate

🚌 Bus 24, 25, 25A

Open: Mon–Sat 0900–1645, Sun 1000–1645

The most twee place in town. The perfect place to bring your grandmother for sandwiches and tea, before indulging in the delights of the cake trolley. Mix of locals and tourists escaping the Royal Mile crowds. Excellent value.

Deli Di Placido 18

36–38 High St

🚌 Bus 5, 7, 14, 14B

Open: Mon–Sat 0800–2000, Sun 1100–1700

Small deli with a selection of Italian treats and a few Scottish oddities thrown in. Some of the best sandwiches in Edinburgh – choose from the likes of spicy chicken and smoked salmon de luxe served up on a variety of breads from *focaccia* to baguettes.

EH1 19

197 High St

🚌 Bus 5, 7, 14, 14B

Open: daily, 0800–0100

Trendy bar/café popular with the city's night-clubbing set. Tasty breakfasts and light lunches make it a good sightseeing stop on the Royal Mile when it is quieter through the day. Tables outside in summer where, during the Festival, you can laze away the afternoon watching the street entertainers perform.

Elephant's Sufficiency 20

170 High St

🚌 Bus 23, 40, 41, 41A

Open: Mon–Fri 0800–1700, Sat–Sun 0900–1700

Relaxed café with good views out on to the Royal Mile offering hearty food. Burgers big enough indeed to satisfy an elephant, with more interesting sandwich

▲ Elephant's Sufficiency

choices such as Atlantic prawn and bacon and Brie. Good array of tempting cakes and coffee to follow the savouries.

The Jolly Judge ㉑

7 James Ct

🚌 Bus 23, 40, 41, 41A

Open: Sun–Thu 1130–2300, Fri–Sat 1130–2300

A cosy bar tucked just off the Royal Mile. Proximity to the Scottish Parliament means that you are often rubbing shoulders with local politicians. Basic pub-grub food served up with a smile and accompanied by a good range of beers. The seats by the fire are a great place to be on a cold day.

Logie Baird's Bar ㉒

The Bank Hotel, 1 South Bridge

🚌 Bus 5, 7, 14, 14B

Open: daily, 0900–0100

Bar that pays tribute to all of Scotland's great inventors and revolutionary thinkers. Typical pub food whose highlight is a good plate of 'haggis, neeps and tatties' laced with whisky sauce. Big leather seats inside and tables outside on the Royal Mile in the warmer months.

Royal Mile Tavern ㉓

127 High St

🚌 Bus 5, 7, 14, 14B

▲ Royal Mile Tavern

Open: Mon–Thu 1100–2300, Fri–Sat 1100–2400, Sun 1230–2300

Old pub laden with bric-à-brac and paintings. Feels as though you have slipped back 50 years and the menu backs this up with traditional pub food on offer, such as steak and Stilton pie and sausage and mash. Hearty if unspectacular.

Southern Cross ㉔

63A Cockburn St

🚌 Bus 5, 7, 14, 14B

Open: Mon–Sat 1100–2300, Sun 1100–1800, closed Mon

Bright café with friendly staff and eye-catching décor, nestling just off the tourist throng of the Royal Mile. The huge club sandwich is the highlight of a light menu that includes some decent salads.

Also a good range of coffees and beer to enjoy in summer at the outdoor tables.

Starbucks ㉕

126 High St

🚌 Bus 5, 7, 14, 14B

Open: Mon–Fri 0730–2100, Sat 0800–2100, Sun 0900–1900

Unthinkable in Edinburgh only ten years ago, this is one of an array of new coffee outlets dotted around the city that have accompanied Edinburgh's 'coffee revolution'. The usual range of coffees that you would expect in this branch of the popular chain. The well-designed interior allows great vantage points for people-watching on the Royal Mile. Sit down or take your coffee and muffins away.

THE ROYAL MILE
Shops, markets and picnic sites

Shops

Fudge House of Edinburgh 26

195 Canongate

⏺ Bus 5, 7, 14, 14B

Open: Mon–Sat 1000–1630,
Sun 1100–1700

The same family has been concocting its tempting sugary treats on the premises for three generations and it is still going strong. Also sells fresh breads and cakes, which are handy for a picnic at the end of the Royal Mile in Holyrood Park.

Holyrood Grocer 27

Holyrood Rd, opp Scotsman
Building

⏺ Bus 24, 25, 25A

Open: daily, 0700–2200

New grocer-cum-super-market right next to the new Scottish Parliament building and Dynamic Earth. An unspectacular range, but opens late so a good place to stock up

▲ Fudge shop

▲ Holyrood Park

on those essentials or to grab a picnic before heading into Holyrood Park. It also stocks the mustards and jams of the legendary Arran Fine Foods.

Jim Garrahy's Fudge Kitchen Ltd 28

30 High St

⏺ Bus 5, 7, 14, 14B

Open: Mon–Fri 1000–1730,
Sat 1000–1800, Sun 1100–1730

While the boast that they make the 'best fudge in the world' may be a little bit of an exaggeration, they do offer a tasty selection of sugary delights. You can even see it being made and snack on the free samples before buying your own. The plain fudge made with fresh cream is divine.

Scottish Grocer 29

297 Canongate

⏺ Bus 5, 7, 14, 14B

Open: daily, 0900–1800

Fresh fruit and basic groceries for a picnic, a rare oasis on the Royal Mile to stock up on all the food and drink essentials, which is especially useful if you are staying at a Royal Mile hotel.

Picnic sites

Holyrood Park 30

⏺ Bus 24, 25 25A

Open: all day

A little bit of the Highlands that hovers just on the edge of the city centre. Sit on a bench by the loch with the spectacular back-drop of a ruined castle and the sweeping Arthur's Seat volcano, and you half expect a clan of kilt-clad Highlanders to descend down the glen. A green oasis that certainly does not feel like a city park.

Business entertainment

Making business pleasurable

In the last decade or so Edinburgh has witnessed the emergence of a new financial district, just a short stroll from the western end of Princes Street. Couple this multi-million-pound project with the renewed confidence that the opening in 1999 of the first Scottish parliament for 300 years has brought, and business is booming in Edinburgh. Accompanying this recent growth there is now a good range of venues, many of them in luxury hotels, for a business lunch or a more formal evening business dinner.

The menu is light and creative and the ambience is of quiet business buzz.

In terms of sheer convenience, though, the Sheraton Grand Hotel is perfectly placed, right at the centre of Edinburgh's new business district. Its **Grill Room** (*1 Festival Sq; ✆ 0131 229 9131; open: Mon–Fri 1200–1430, 1900–2230, Sat 1900–2230, closed Sun; ❸❸❸; reservations advised*) has won awards for the high standard of its cuisine and is a firm favourite of the Lothian Road business crowd. Scottish paintings adorn the walls and traditional Scottish cuisine graces the menu. The Grill Room is on the pricey side, but it offers an excellent value lunch menu, with wine included.

Just a short stroll down Lothian Road brings you to the Caledonian Hilton Hotel, which boasts another excellent restaurant for business people, **Pompadour** (*Princes St; ✆ 0131 459 9988; open: Tue–Sat 1230–1430, 1900–2230, closed Sun–Mon; ❸❸❸; reservations advised*). This classy eatery has a reputation for formality and indeed it makes the perfect venue for impressing clients in the evening, but it also affords a lighter, sprightlier lunch menu for that all-important business lunch. Downstairs, on the lobby level, **Chisholm's** is a much more relaxed bistro-style restaurant (*see page 39*).

At the far end of Princes Sreet, Edinburgh's other grand city hotel, the Balmoral, also impresses, with its **Number One** restaurant (*1 Princes St; ✆ 0131 557 6727; open: Mon–Fri 1200–1430, 1900–2130, Sat–Sun 1900–2130; ❸❸❸; reservations essential*). The ambience is far more modern than Pompadour, but the service is as immaculate and the cuisine is singularly impressive.

Another numerically named restaurant is **No. 36** (*36 Great King St; ✆ 0131 556 3636; open: daily 1900–2200, ❶❷; reservations advisable*), beneath the stately Howard Hotel. It may have stopped serving lunches during the week, but it still offers one of the city's most innovative venues for dinner, with funky, modern architecture and cuisine.

Owned by the same people behind No. 36, the Townhouse Company, **Channings** (*12–16 South Learmonth Gdns; ✆ 0131 315 2225; open: daily 1230–1400, 1830–2130, ❶❷; reservations advisable*) is arguably the best place in the city for a business lunch. Break away from the city centre and cross over Dean Bridge to this oasis of calm hidden away in a Georgian townhouse. The menu is light and creative and the ambience is of quiet business buzz. If you are counting your expenses, Channings also offers very good value.

Edinburgh sees a substantial amount of business coming in from the Far East to visit both the city itself and the nearby 'Silicon Glen' around the satellite town of Livingston. Until the middle of 1999 this market was well catered for by the legendary Darumya's Japanese restaurant, down in Leith's Commercial Quay. Fortunately, a decent Japanese alternative still exists just on the edge of the city centre in the form of **Yumi's** (*2 West Coates; ✆ 0131 337 2173; open: Mon–Sat 1830–2300, closed Sun; ❶❷; reservations advisable*). Its sushi attracts a steady following of locals and this is the first port of call for many visiting Far Eastern businessmen. Quiet surrounds and unobtrusive service is conducive to a business lunch where the emphasis is on getting things done.

If you are looking to organise a larger scale lunch meeting or a conference with food, then most of Edinburgh's larger hotels will be able to help. A cosier alternative is to book the **Cabinet Room** at the Parliament House Hotel (*15 Calton Hill; ✆ 0131 478 4000; www.scotland-hotels.co.uk*). This boutique-style hotel is tucked away in a quiet location near Calton Hill and enjoys fine views down across to the Firth of Forth. It has a capacity of up to 40 delegates and is flexible to differing culinary requirements.

The Old Town

Nestling in the shadow of the castle, the Grassmarket lies at the centre of the Old Town. Renowned as the best venue for a pub crawl around its numerous pubs, there is also a good choice of eating venues, both on the Grassmarket itself and in the medieval streets around the rest of the Old Town.

THE OLD TOWN
Restaurants

bleu ❶

36–38 Victoria St

⌀ 0131 226 1900

🚌 Bus 23, 40, 41, 41A

Open: daily, 1200–1500, 1800–2300

Reservations recommended

[VISA] 💳

French

€

Twin of the bleu down on Union St (*see page 69*) and offering the same type of French cuisine, this is definitely the more intimate restaurant of the two and it has a surprisingly more relaxed ambience given the similarity of the menu. Enjoy the French-fusion food in small *bouchées* or larger servings as the owners successfully weld French cuisine and inimitable Spanish *tapas*-style food together.

Caffè Romano ❷

110 West Bow

⌀ 0131 225 5028

🚌 Bus 2, 40, 41, 41A

Open: Mon–Thu 1200–1430, 1700–2200, Fri–Sat 1200–2200, Sun 1700–2200

Reservations recommended

[VISA] 💳

Italian

€

This place does not feel too much like an Italian restaurant, but the food is authentic, with all the usual Italian main-stays that you would expect done well. The set lunch menus in particular are excellent value and set you up for the afternoon.

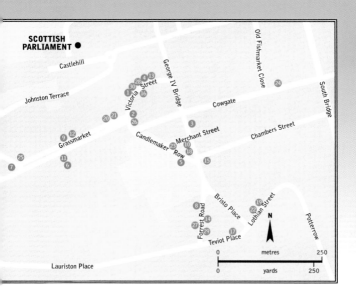

Dial ③

44–46 George IV Bridge

✆ 0131 225 7179

🚌 Bus 40, 41, 41A

Open: Mon–Sat 1200–1500,
1800–2300, Sun 1200–
1500, 1900–2300

Reservations recommended

VISA 💳 American Express

Modern Scottish

❶❷

Trendy venue which
reflects the style of the
food. The eating 'space'
looks like the interior of
some designer-style
hotel and complements
the food, which looks
just as good. The menu
is continually innova-
tive and interesting,
with Scottish produce
given unique twists.

▲ Enjoying Scottish cuisine

Two-floored Mexican that dubiously styles itself as 'The Best Little Haw House' in the east. Decide for yourself, but what it undoubtedly does offer are all of the reliable Mexican staples. The service are friendly and the atmosphere relaxed in an eatery that is handily located near the numerous pubs of the Grassmarket.

The Heights ❻

Apex International Hotel, 31–35 The Grassmarket

∅ 0131 300 3456

🚌 Bus 2

Open: daily, 1200–1430, 1900–2130

Reservations essential

All credit cards accepted

Scottish

❻❻

Even if the food was terrible, people would still flock here just to soak up the sweeping views of the Grassmarket below and the castle perched high above. Thankfully the food is a worthwhile accompaniment, even if The Heights may not offer the most exciting menu in the city. The views make it the perfect setting for a first night in town or a romantic dinner for two, but make sure you book a window table in advance.

Helios ❼

7 The Grassmarket

∅ 0131 229 7884

🚌 Bus 2

The Grain Store ❹

30 Victoria St

∅ 0131 225 7635

🚌 Bus 23, 40, 41, 41A

Open: Mon–Thu 1200–1400, 1800–2000, Fri–Sat 1200–1500, 1800–2300, Sun 1200–1500

Reservations recommended

VISA 💳 American Express

Scottish

❻❻

Good vantage point to watch the street life below. The food veers towards the traditional side with only a few innovations popping up in starters and desserts, but the Grain Store is the perfect place if you are looking for solid Scottish cooking.

Haw House ❺

44 Candlemaker Row

∅ 0131 220 4420

🚌 Bus 2, 40, 41, 41A

Open: Mon–Thu 1730–1130, Fri–Sun 1200–1500, 1730–2400

Reservations recommended

VISA 💳 American Express

Mexican

❻❻

Open: Mon–Sat 1000–1800, Sun 1200–1700

Reservations recommended

No credit cards accepted

Vegetarian

Wade through the small shop at the western end of the Grassmarket to discover the great little eatery hiding through the back. Perch at the wooden tables and fill yourself up with the excellent vegetarian specials. With no music or fussy service you are left alone to unwind away from the rest of the bustling Grassmarket.

Maharajas ⑧

17–19 Forrest Rd

✆ 0131 220 2273

🚌 Bus 23, 40, 41, 41A

Open: daily, 1200–1330, 1730–2330

Reservations recommended

Indian

The décor is all very Raj and pleasantly tacky at the same time. This award-winning restaurant is one of the city's better Indian eateries. Some dishes err on the side of blandness, but the food is good value and the spicy baltis are delicious.

Mamma's ⑨

30 The Grassmarket

✆ 0131 225 6464

🚌 Bus 2

Open: Sun–Thu 1200–2300, Fri–Sat 1200–2400

Reservations recommended

American

Massive choice of excellent pizzas in this restaurant that looks as though it has been flown straight in from

the American mid-West. Always busy with tourists, families and even local businessmen flocking to sample some of the best pizzas in town and the tempting dessert choices. Getting the big plastic blue-and-white checked tablecloths messy is all part of the fun.

Merchants ⑩

17 Merchant St

✆ 0131 225 4009

🚌 Bus 2, 23, 40, 41, 41A

Open: Mon–Fri 1200–1400, 1800–2200, Sat 1800–2200, closed Sun

Reservations recommended

All credit cards accepted

Scottish

If you are in the mood for a hearty Scots meal served up in convivial surrounds, then this is a great place to head. Savour a pre-dinner

▲ Mamma's

whisky in the armchairs or at the bar, before loosening your belt to take in the filling food on offer. The traditional music and the Scottish hospitality may not always please all of the locals, but they are much more attractive to adventurous tourists taking a detour.

Metro ⓫

Apex International Hotel, 31–35 The Grassmarket

✆ 0131 300 3456

🚌 Bus 2

Open: daily, 1200–1430, 1900–2145

Reservations essential

All credit cards accepted

International

❻

A more bright and breezy eatery in the same hotel as **The Heights** restaurant (*see page 20*). This smaller sibling is a good alternative to the pub lunches that dominate elsewhere in the Grassmarket.

Petit Paris ⓬

38–40 The Grassmarket

✆ 0131 226 2442

🚌 Bus 2

Open: daily, 1200–1500, 1730–2300

Reservations recommended

All credit cards accepted

French

❻

Intimate restaurant serving traditional French dishes. Large portions are the norm and the excellent *moules marinières* are

no exception. On the dessert menu choose from crêpes, crêpes and yet more crêpes.

Pierre Victoire ⓭

10 Victoria St

✆ 0131 225 1721

🚌 Bus 23, 40, 41, 41A

Open: daily, 1200–1500, 1800–2300

Reservations recommended

💳 💶

French

❻

Pierre Victoire was once one of Edinburgh's great culinary success stories, building an empire admirably based on tasty French bistro cooking at an affordable price. Sadly, the business overstretched itself and collapsed and this is one of the few remaining branches of the now-defunct chain to keep the original name. Expect sturdy French bistro-style cooking and the excellent value set lunch menus that were the cornerstone of the Pierre Victoire empire.

Tapas Olé ⓮

4A Forrest Rd

✆ 0131 225 7069

🚌 Bus 23, 40, 41, 41A

Open: Mon–Thu 1200–2230, Fri–Sat 1200–2400, Sun 1530–2230

All credit cards accepted

Spanish

❻

Seville comes to Edinburgh with a fairly authentic stab at *tapas*.

A great place to come if you are in a group as you can all choose something off the menu and then share the plates around. The *chorizo* is delicious and spiced just as it should be. Very lively atmosphere in the evenings as office groups come in to relax after work.

The Tower ⓯

Museum of Scotland, Chambers St

✆ 0131 225 3003

🚌 Bus 23, 40, 41, 41A

Open: Mon–Sat 1000–2300, Sun 1200–2300

Reservations recommended

All credit cards accepted

Scottish

❻❻

Modern Scottish at its best served in the stunning new Museum of Scotland (when the museum itself is closed, enter through the main Museum door and take the lift to the restaurant). Good choice of tasty, light meals presented with style and panache. Stunning views of the castle perched high above the city and food to match. Very funky décor and surprisingly comfortable seats that look as though they have been brought in from the pages of a South Beach fashion shoot. Visit for lunch to enjoy the castle when it is occasionally bathed in sunshine and return at night to see the city sparkle.

THE OLD TOWN
Bars, cafés and pubs

Baracoa 16

7 Victoria St

🚍 Bus 23, 40, 41, 41A

Open: daily, 1100–0100

Delve into Baracoa and prepare to be transported to pre-Castro Cuba. This bar does veer on the tacky side of things, with huge flags and big fans, but its food is worth coming in for. Many come to try the wide range of cocktails and the twice-weekly salsa classes, but exotic dishes such as chicken in a rich coconut sauce and roast ham basted in mustard, cider and mango are also an atttraction.

Bookstop Café 17

4 Teviot Place

🚍 Bus 23, 40, 41, 41A

Open: Mon–Sat 1000–1930, Sun 1130–1930

Reflecting the arty nature of the area, this small café doubles up as a bookshop. Unsurprisingly, students flock here to thumb through their books and sample the excellent coffees and the small range of light snacks and sandwiches.

Elephant House 18

21 George IV Bridge

🚍 Bus 23, 40, 41, 41A

Open: Mon–Fri 0800–2300, Sat–Sun 1000–2300

Consistently voted by locals as the city's finest café, the Elephant House rarely disappoints. Leaf through the newspapers, indulge in the extensive range of teas and coffees, but most of all savour the fresh range of salads and quiches and tempting array of cakes. If you are lucky, you may even manage to grab one of the coveted seats in the back room, which offer impressive views of the castle.

Iguana 19

41 Lothian St

🚍 Bus 23, 40, 41, 41A

Open: daily, 0900–0100

It may be frequented by students from the University across the road, but this classy café/bar offers a real alternative to Edinburgh's restaurants. The bright, modern décor complements well the bright, modern food with lively options that take their cues from the Pacific Rim.

▲ The Last Drop

▲ OZ Bar

The Last Drop 20

74 The Grassmarket

🚌 Bus 2

Open: Mon–Sat 1100–0100, Sun 1230–0100

An atmospheric touristy pub on the site where the city used to hang its villains. Sturdy pub food with a good range of beers and whiskies, and a hot toddy to warm you up on a cold day.

Maggie Dickson's Pub 21

92 The Grassmarket

🚌 Bus 2

Open: daily, 1100–0100

Named after the bizarre story of a suspected witch who survived her spell at the gallows. The pub grub is basic, with fish and chips and various simple meals, but the sinister, gothic atmosphere is worth a visit for a low-priced lunch.

Negociants 22

45–47 Lothian St

🚌 Bus 23, 40, 41, 41A

Open: daily, 0900–0300

Late-opening continental-style bar/café at the heart of Edinburgh University's main campus. Negociants is more than just a student drinking den, offering a wide range of tasty snacks and full meals, which are especially handy late at night when the city's restaurants close. The outside tables during the summer months are an Edinburgh institution.

OZ Bar 23

33 Candlemaker Row

🚌 Bus 23, 40, 41, 41A

Open: Mon–Thu 1200–2400, Fri–Sat 1200–0100, Sun 1200–2300

Edinburgh's original Australian theme bar is still going strong. Here you will find some hearty meals with the unusual appearance on an Edinburgh menu of kangaroo.

Siglo 24

184 Cowgate

🚌 Bus 5, 7, 14, 14B

Open: Sun–Thu 1200–2400, Fri–Sat 1200–0100

Funky new Spanish-themed bar/café on the Cowgate. Bright interior and good range of freshly prepared Spanish staples. It gets its *serrano* ham from **Lupe Pinto's Deli** (*see page 54*), so the quality is guaranteed. One of the few bars in town selling the Spanish Cruzcampo beer. Live music and DJs at night.

Three Quarters Sports Café 25

4 The Grassmarket

🚌 Bus 2

Open: Mon–Sat 1100–0100, Sun 1230–0100

This bar/café is the best place in town to catch the biggest sports events, especially rugby matches, as it is owned by some ex-Scotland players. Most people flock here to quaff beer as they watch the big games, but food is always served and you can book tables ahead to ensure a seat no matter how busy it gets. Simple menu with big burgers, platters to share and occasional daily specials.

THE OLD TOWN
Shops, markets and picnic sites

Shops

The Cooks Bookshop 26

118 West Bow

🚌 Bus 2

Open: Mon–Sat 1030–1730, closed Sun

Small bookshop stuffed full of cookbooks covering all types of cuisines. If you are interested in cooking your own Scottish food when you get back home you can stock up here on both traditional and more modern recipes.

Flowers Fresh Fruit 27

43 Forrest Rd

🚌 Bus 23, 40, 41, 41A

Open: Mon–Fri 0800–1700, closed Sat–Sun

One of the few places in the Old Town to stock fresh fruit and vegetables in a small shop that you will miss if you blink for a second.

I J Mellis Cheesemonger 28

30A Victoria St

🚌 Bus 23, 40, 41, 41A

Open: Mon–Sat 0930–1830, Sun 1000–1700

Famous cheesemonger who takes the best young cheese from farmers in Scotland and Ireland and ripens them on site. You will find his tasty creations featured on menus throughout the city, and if you ask any chef to recommend a good cheesemonger the chances are that you will be directed here. Mellis stocks an excellent range of cheeses and the friendly staff are always willing to help dedicated cheese lovers and the curious alike.

Rudi Deli 29

30 Forrest Rd

🚌 Bus 23, 40, 41, 41A

Open: Mon–Fri 0930–1730, Sat 0930–1500, closed Sun

Tiny deli just over from the city's main university campus. Very good range of coffee beans, teas and Italian sauces, as well as pastries, *pain au chocolat* and croissants. The deli stocks the legendary Baxters soups from Speyside and also has some interesting Bavarian rye breads that are brought in daily from Glasgow.

▲ I J Mellis Cheesemonger

La Sologne 30

30 Victoria St

🚌 Bus 23, 40, 41, 41A

Open: Mon–Fri 0830–1800, Sat 0830–1730, Sun 1100–1630

Small French/Scottish food emporium tucked into Victoria Street just off the Grassmarket. It boasts that half of the produce on sale is homemade. Amongst the crammed shelves you will find its own-brand pâtés, *confits*, jams, chutneys and jellies.

▲ La Sologne

Traditional Edinburgh pubs

Fancy a tipple or two?

It is an oft-quoted boast amongst Edinburgh's proud locals that their city has more pubs per capita than anywhere else in the world. After a night spent exploring the city's hostelries you will probably not be in much of a mood to argue with these claims. Over the last few years the more dedicated of Edinburgh's drinkers have begun to bemoan the string of bright new modern bar/cafés that have sprung up across the city. They worry that this trend will kill the old drinking dens, but there are still plenty of these around to give you a real taste of the traditional Edinburgh drinking culture.

> **It is an oft-quoted boast amongst Edinburgh's proud locals that their city has more pubs per capita than anywhere else in the world.**

It is wise when visiting any of these pubs not to flash around your money and to keep an eye on your belongings, though there are very rarely any problems for tourist visitors, who are usually given a warm welcome. Also bear in mind that these pubs are an integral part of many of the drinkers' lives and, unsurprisingly, they are not too keen on having cameras and camcorders shoved in their faces.

The food on offer in these establishments can usually be best described as basic pub grub. Expect a stack of filled rolls, with basic fillings such as cheese and butter (no *focaccia* or sun-dried tomatoes here), pies and possibly stovies, as well as – sometimes – a more lengthy menu at lunchtimes.

One of the best places to start your alcoholic exploration is at the **Fiddlers Arms** (*9–11 The Grassmarket*), which is well used to curious tourists. Adorning the walls is a myriad of all types of fiddles, but propping up the bar is a far more interesting array of characters. The décor is pleasantly shabby and a world away from the other tourist-orientated pubs in the Grassmarket. Grab your cheese roll here and wash it down with a pint of heavy to taste a slice of real Edinburgh.

Down in the West End **Mathers** (*1 Queensferry St*) is another traditional bar that has somehow managed to survive the modernisation that has swamped the hostelries all around. Here you will find a good crowd of regulars, who range from local students right through to businessmen sneaking out of the sterile bar/cafés to grab a lunchtime pint. Another Mathers bar is somehow still managing to survive intact on trendy Broughton Street.

If you find that you are really developing a taste for heavy ale during your visit to Edinburgh then make for **Diggers** (*1 Angle Park Terrace*), which many locals reckon has the best pint of McEwans 80/- in the city. Grab a pint, a meat pie and try to blend in with the Tynecastle faithful who flock here before big football matches to fill up their bellies with beer before cheering on Heart of Midlothian.

Over at the other end of town the supporters of Hibernian, the second of the city's two big football clubs, gather at **Robbie's** (*367 Leith Walk*) for a pre- or post-match pint and a hauf. Robbie's is one of the string of rough-and-ready men's pubs on Leith Walk that it is safe to take your partner to. From the comfort of your pint glass you can watch the minutiae of Edinburgh life in a scene that is as captivating as any movie, though it is admittedly more *Trainspotting* than *Braveheart*.

The **Oxford Bar** (*98 Young St*) may sound like the sort of classy joint you would expect so close to increasingly posh George Street, but the reality couldn't be more different. How the Oxford survives right at the heart of the city centre is a constant source of amazement, as are the great pints of heavy, the best you will find this close to Princes Street.

If a big rugby match is on, then watch Edinburgh come together at the **Roseburn Bar** (*1 Roseburn Terrace*). On match days all pretensions and class divisions are thrown out of the window as young mobile phone-clad executives and company managing directors rub shoulders with old ladies mumbling away in anoraks and gruff old men cursing that their stovies are too cold.

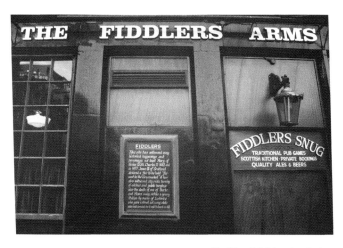

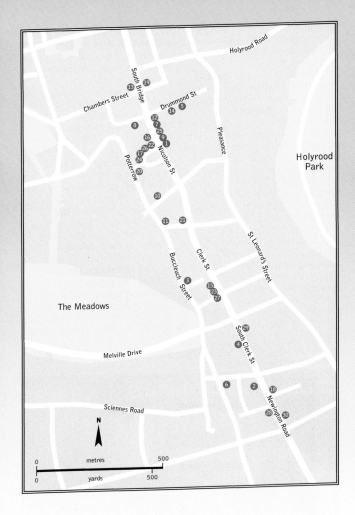

South Bridge and Newington

The south side of the city may be a little off the main tourist routes, but heading south from the old heart of the city you will find a range of good-value restaurants, bars and informal eateries that cater for Edinburgh's large student community, as well as a few fine dining options.

SOUTH BRIDGE AND NEWINGTON
Restaurants

Ayutthaya ❶

14B Nicolson St

✆ 0131 556 9351

🚍 Bus 7, 8, 14, 31, 33, 82

Open: daily, 1200–1430, 1700–2300

Reservations recommended

All credit cards accepted

Thai

€

Easy stop for those not *au fait* with Thai cooking. The menu explains in detail what you are getting so you won't end up having your taste buds blown off by the chillies. And what you are getting is above par Thai food in cosy surroundings, served with a smile.

Banks Grill Room and Restaurant ❷

10 Newington Rd

✆ 0131 667 0707

🚍 Bus 7, 8, 14, 31, 33, 82

Open: Tues–Sat 1200–2430, 1800–2200, Sun 1230–2200 (Grill Room only)

Reservations recommended

American Express

Traditional/modern Scottish

€ €

Diners can feast on one of the tempting steaks that are dished up in the Grill Room. With a variety of cuts and sizes (the largest a whopping 16oz) served with different sauces, there is usually something to satisfy everyone.

Alternatively, eat in the à la carte restaurant, where game, fish and poultry spring up on the menu.

La Bonne Mer ❸

113 Buccleuch St

✆ 0131 662 9111

🚍 Bus 7, 8, 14, 31, 33, 82

Open: Tue–Sat 1200–1400, 1800–2200, closed Sun–Mon

Reservations recommended

American Express

Seafood

€

Right at the heart of Edinburgh's main university campus, this seafood restaurant is not just for students and

▲ Susie's Wholefood Diner

tutors. Unlike Leith's seafood restaurants, there is not too much of an attempt to create a nautical atmosphere, just simple, well-presented seafood.

Dragon Way ❹

74–78 South Clerk St

✆ 0131 668 1328

🚍 Bus 7, 8, 14, 31, 33, 82

Open: Mon–Fri 1200–1430, 1700–2400, Sat 1700–2400, Sun 1800–2400

Reservations recommended

All credit cards accepted

Chinese

❻

Hong Kong cuisine comes to Edinburgh in a restaurant that you leave expecting to stroll on to Victoria Harbour. The chef specialises in Cantonese cuisine, but switches provinces a couple of times on the menu to rustle up some fine Szechuan offerings.

Khushi's ❺

16 Drummond St

✆ 0131 556 8996

🚍 Bus 7, 8, 14, 31, 33, 82

Open: Sun–Thu 1200–1500, 1700–2100, Fri–Sat 1200–1500, 1700–2130

Reservations not allowed

No credit cards accepted

Indian

❻

A real institution on the Edinburgh restaurant scene, Khushi's has been around since it first brought Indian food to the city in 1947. Cheap and cheerful with none of the paraphernalia and tackiness of many ethnic eateries. Feels like a university canteen, a feeling accentuated by the students from the nearby university.

Unusually for Edinburgh, it is also BYOB and there is no corkage charge. If you have not brought any alcohol along then pop to the pub next door, which seems to have an informal arrangement for supplying drinks to Khushi's diners.

The Marque ❻

19–21 Causewayside

✆ 0131 466 6660

🚍 Bus 7, 8, 14, 31, 33, 82

Open: Tues–Thu 1145–1400, 1745–2200, Fri 1145–1400, 1745–2300, Sat 1230–1400, 1745–2300, Sun 1230–1400, 1745–2200, closed Mon

Reservations recommended

💳 American Express

Scottish

❻❻

Top-class cuisine served in a very homely environment where genuine friendliness replaces silver service. The ever-changing menu draws heavily on seafood.

Nicolson's Restaurant ❼

6A Nicolson St

✆ 0131 557 4567

🚍 Bus 7, 8, 14, 31, 33, 82

Open: Mon–Fri 1200–1500, 1700–2300, Sat–Sun 1200–2400

Reservations unnecessary

💳

Mediterranean

❻❻

Looks more like the trendy Scandinavian furniture store, IKEA,

than a restaurant. Smart colours, big windows and quick service work well in this bistro just off the main tourist centre. Many people just pop in for drinks and a snack before hopping over to the nearby Festival Theatre, but those that do miss out on a menu which is worth an evening on its own.

Off the Wall ❽

11 South College St

✆ 0131 667 1597

🚍 Bus 7, 8, 14, 31, 33, 82

Open: Mon–Sat 1200–1400, 1730–2300, closed Sun

Reservations essential

💳 American Express

Modern Scottish

❻❻❻

Unlikely no-frills setting for food of such excellence. Forget the lack of pleasing décor and the informality of the service and just enjoy the fresh Scottish produce given innovative twists in this tiny restaurant tucked just off the main tourist district. Great **Ian Mellis** cheeseboard (*see page 24*) and full of locals. Their steaks are divine.

Suruchi ❾

14A Nicolson St

✆ 0131 556 6583

🚍 Bus 7, 8, 14, 31, 33, 82

Open: Mon–Sat 1200–1400, 1730–2330, Sun 1730–2330

Reservations recommended

💳 American Express

Indian

❻

A cultural as well as a culinary experience in an Indian restaurant that insists on its menu being printed in the 'Scots' language. Some of the locals struggle as much as the tourists, but the staff are on hand to help and the food is worth the linguistic labours.

Susie's Wholefood Diner ❿

51–53 West Nicolson St

✆ 0131 667 8729

🚍 Bus 7, 8, 14, 31, 33, 82

Open: Mon 0900–2000, Tues–Sat 0900–2100, Sun 1230–1800

Reservations unnecessary

No credit cards accepted

Vegetarian

❻

Excellent vegetarian restaurant just over from Edinburgh University's main campus. Choose from a normal or large plate and watch it being heaped full of tasty mains like vegetarian lasagne and Spanish tortilla, as well as lashings of fresh and interesting salads. Homely down-at-heel ambience makes it a relaxing venue for lunch. Worth a visit alone to test its claim to have the 'best *falafel* in the world'.

SOUTH BRIDGE AND NEWINGTON
Bars, cafés and pubs

Bar ce lona 🄫

2–8 West Crosscauseway

🄫 Bus 7, 8, 14, 31, 33, 82

Open: daily, 1100–0100

A bright modern bar that is popular with the local student community. The food focuses around the Mediterranean with pizzas, *panini* and big, fresh salads. Live DJs at weekends make it a good place to grab a quick meal as you get into the mood for a big night out on the town.

Black Medicine 🄬

2 Nicolson St

🄫 Bus 7, 8, 14, 31, 33, 82

Open: daily, 0800–2000

A real coffee emporium laden with numerous varieties of the hallowed bean as well as 'Edinburgh Blend' tea. A good place to grab a coffee and snack before popping over the road to the Festival Theatre.

Brasserie No. 1 🄭

1 Chambers St

🄫 Bus 7, 8, 14, 31, 33, 82

Open: Sun–Wed 0815–2300, Thu–Sat 0815–0300

All-day menu in this big, bright brasserie just a short stroll from the Chambers St museums.

Join the students who flock here to feast up on the filling fodder. It also has cheap drinks on Friday nights and live jazz on Saturday.

Café Aquarius 🄮

10 Drummond St

🄫 Bus 7, 8, 14, 31, 33, 82

Open: Mon–Thu 1100–2300, Fri–Sat 1100–0100, Sun 1700–2300

Step back a couple of decades to a world of flares and disco in this 1970s-style bar/café. Very popular with the pre-clubbing set, with DJs at weekends and the lively Cowgate a stagger away. Café Aquarius also produces some great food. Choose from sandwiches and salads, as well as more sophisticated main courses.

Caffè Europa 🄯

53 Clerk St

🄫 Bus 7, 8, 14, 31, 33, 82

Open: Mon–Thu 0930–2230, Fri–Sat 0930–2130, closed Sun

Lebanese-owned eatery that spreads its culinary wings wider. Yes, it does have olive oil-laden Mediterranean treats, but it also offers steaks and a good selection of desserts. It is also the only eatery in town to

▲ Wok Bar

offer a separate Lebanese menu. Look out also for the lunch specials, which include a glass of the house plonk.

City Restaurant 16

33–35 Nicolson St

Bus 7, 8, 14, 31, 33, 82

Open: daily, 0800–0100

Not for the faint-hearted or those watching their waistlines, this unreconstructed, shabby place is a favourite of many locals. Deep-fried everything is the order of the day, with a couple of Italian dishes thrown on to the menu as a failed attempt at a healthy balance. If you want to eat like the locals who can't afford the big name restaurants then this is the venue for a down-to-earth eating experience.

Kebab Mahal 17

7 Nicolson Sq

Bus 7, 8, 14, 31, 33, 82

Open: Mon–Thu 1200–0100, Fri–Sat 1200–0200, Sun 1200–2400

Arguably Edinburgh's best Indian halal takeaway, you will find curries and kebabs to die for here, as well as fantastic biriyanis. Popular with the student and post-pub crowds for its great value food. Basic seats are available if you want to sit down.

Metropole 18

33 Newington Rd

Bus 7, 8, 14, 31, 33, 82

Open: daily, 0900–2200

Yet another bank conversion in a city overflowing with them. Massive range of teas and coffees keep the locals coming back for more and hungry visitors can enjoy the range of bagels, sandwiches and nachos, as well as the customary café cakes and muffins. A good place to relax, very feng shui, with a trickling fountain, mirrors and leafy plants.

Oxygen Bar 19

3–5 Infirmary St

Bus 7, 8, 14, 31, 33, 82

Open: daily, 1000–0100

Oxygen is the gimmick and reputedly great after a night of too much culinary and alcoholic indulgence. This bar also does good bar snacks and has a decent restaurant attached with fresh and innovative cuisine.

Wok Bar 20

26–31 Potterrow

Bus 7, 8, 14, 31, 33, 82

Open: Sun–Wed 1100–2300, Thu–Sat 1100–2400

Bright new bar/café that specialises in Asian food. Choose from curries, grills and ramen noodle soups, all very reasonable priced. A healthy option for a quick lunch along with Edinburgh's student community who know a good deal when they see it.

SOUTH BRIDGE AND NEWINGTON
Shops, markets and picnic sites

Shops

Aihua 21

36 West Crosscauseway

🚌 Bus 7, 8, 14, 31, 33, 82

Open: Mon–Wed, Fri–Sat 1000–1900, Thu 1300–1900, Sun 1030–1800

One of Edinburgh's few Chinese supermarkets in a city that does not have its own Chinatown as such. It stocks a good range of Chinese groceries and this is a great place to pick-up exotic spices, though it is a bit short on fresh produce.

Bismillah 22

3 Nicolson Sq

🚌 Bus 7, 8, 14, 31, 33, 82

Open: daily, 1000–2130

Small ethnic grocer selling a limited selection of food stuffs, with a huge selection of spices and tasty baklava desserts sold by weight.

Bonningtons 23

75 Clerk St

🚌 Bus 7, 8, 14, 31, 33, 82

Open: Mon–Sat 0830–1730, closed Sun

Bonningtons has well-stocked cheese and cooked-meat counters, which are manned by friendly and knowledge-able staff. A wide range of fresh bread is on display in the window. Also on offer are various continental breads, Baxters soup and Macsweens haggis. Bonningtons is the most serious foodie-type shop in this area of town.

Elephants & Bagels 24

37 Marshall St

🚌 Bus 7, 8, 14, 31, 33, 82

Open: Mon–Fri 0830–1800, Sat–Sun 1000–1700

Owned by the same people behind the famed Elephant House café in the Old Town (see page 22), this is the place in Edinburgh to buy your bagels. Pre-filled bagels are available, and you can eat in, but many people come just to snap up the wide range of plain and flavoured bagels. This is definitely

elephants & bagels

Edinburgh's first & foremost authentic Bagel & Sandwich shop

Dazed and Confused?

Why not try one of our full Breakfast Bagels?

Scrambled Egg, Juicy Bacon & Tomato on a deliciously filling toasted Bagel.

THE BEST HANGOVER CURE IN EDINBURGH!

Nicholson Square, Edinburgh
Tel. 0131 668 4404

the best place for devoted bagel lovers.

Jordan Valley Health Foods ㉕

8 Nicolson St

🚍 Bus 7, 8, 14, 31, 33, 82

Open: Mon–Fri 0900–1900, Sat 1100–1800, closed Sun

If you are looking for somewhere to stock up on healthy food, then this is the place, in a street that overflows with greasy fast-food outlets. They boast a wide range of products, with the homemade pâtés, yoghurts and dips particularly worth seeking out. For the sweet-toothed they still have the indulgence of baklava cakes.

Mahir Store ㉖

10 Nicolson Sq

🚍 Bus 7, 8, 14, 31, 33, 82

Open: daily, 1000–2230

Asia, Africa and Arabia come to Edinburgh with this ethnic grocer. Crammed into this tiny shop is also a decent range of fresh fruits and vegetables, as well as halal meat.

Nature's Gate ㉗

83 Clerk St

🚍 Bus 7, 8, 14, 31, 33, 82

Open: Mon–Sat 1000–1900, Sun 1200–1600

This is a well-stocked health food shop. Choose from the likes of tofu and honey and an extensive range of herbs and spices. The Scottish fruit wines are worth buying for the novelty value alone, though they won't have many New World wine producers quaking in their boots.

Roots Wholefoods ㉘

60 Newington Rd

🚍 Bus 7, 8, 14, 31, 33, 82

Open: 0900–1800, closed Sun

Roots is a health-food shop with a deli counter tucked in a back room. It stocks a wide range of peas, beans, couscous, dried fruits and the like, as well as porridge oats by weight, which under-cuts supermarket prices. Like many health food shops in Edinburgh, it stocks Macsweens vegetarian haggis.

Sandwich Filling Station ㉙

39 South Clerk St

🚍 Bus 7, 8, 14, 31, 33, 82

Open: Mon–Sat 0830–1830, Sun 1100–1600

Impossibly small deli always impossibly crammed with customers and for good reason. This is a good place to sample savouries and sandwich fillings, as well as the range of sugary delights that tempt in the window display. Be prepared to queue.

Sey's New York Deli ㉚

59 Newington Rd

🚍 Bus 7, 8, 14, 31, 33, 82

Open: Mon–Fri 0700–1700, Sat 0900–1700, Sun 1000–1500

Great little deli tucked right down on Newington Road, well away from tourist Edinburgh. Big, juicy olives, pastrami, Parma ham and *chorizo* amongst many other attractions, without the inflated prices that often accompany decent continental food. Also good bread and a great place to purchase picnic treats.

Heavy ales

A brew to savour

The idea of savouring a large pint of lukewarm ale for fun may seem an alien concept to visitors from sunnier climes more used to a short glass of ice-cold beer. You cannot really say you have visited Edinburgh, however, unless you have tried the 'heavy' ales beloved of the locals.

Heavy is named according to its strength, with the most popular varieties 70/- (pronounced 'seventy schilling') and the slightly stronger 80/-. The ale is usually served at cellar temperature and hand-pumped uncarbonated from a cask.

There has recently been a furore as some of the big breweries are rumoured to have reduced the alcoholic content in an attempt to save money, with purists claiming that this will drastically alter the taste. The

fuss generated by this reveals the strong feelings that heavy drinkers have for their hallowed tipple.

Although lagers (beer to most New Worlders) are increasingly popular throughout Edinburgh, there are still many producers of heavy. The big boys are Youngers, McEwans and Tennants, though there are smaller producers such as Caledonian and Belhaven, whose products are just as good, if not better.

To get right to the heart of heavy, make straight for the **Caley Sample Room** (*5–8 Angle Park Terrace*). Owned by the adjacent Caledonian Brewery, it sells a good range of the Brewery's own ales as well as a few guest selections thrown in for good measure. You can try the basic pub lunches, but people come here principally to sample the alcoholic delights.

The **Caledonian Ale House** (*1–3 Haymarket Terrace*) has a traditional bar downstairs, serving all the usual heavy ales in pleasant surroundings. If you are hungry, there is also a grill room upstairs that moves beyond simple pub grub towards bistro-style Scottish cooking.

A good bet for a decent pint of heavy in the heart of tourist Edinburgh is at the **Bow Bar** (*80 West Bow*) on picturesque Victoria Street. Here you may not

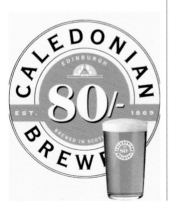

be the only tourist by any means, but the pints are still of an excellent quality. It also stocks a great range of single malt whiskies so it is the perfect chance to join the locals and order a 'pint and a hauf'.

The **Guildford Arms** (*1 West Register St*) is a big, brash Victorian affair, a universe away from some of the more traditional drinking dens where you will find good ale in Edinburgh. It has a massive range of great ales from which to choose and features decent pub food – and all this just a two-minute walk from Princes Street.

One of the most atmospheric venues for quaffing fine ale is down in the bowels of the Cowgate at **Bannermans** (*212 The Cowgate*). This cave-like bar is all low ceilings and stone walls, which adds to the ambience. Legend has it that it used to operate a system that meant if you could drink all of the ales along the bar then you could drink your way back for free, but with a clientele of students, and particularly the Edinburgh

> **You cannot really say you have visited Edinburgh unless you have tried the 'heavy' ales beloved of the locals.**

University rugby team, this proved to be a very dangerous offer and was soon stopped before the bar went bust!

If you are travelling with a family and do not feel comfortable taking the little ones into some of Edinburgh's earthier bars – many will not allow you to anyway – then make for Newhaven and the welcoming arms of the **Starbank Inn** (*64 Laverbank Rd*). Here you can savour some excellent ales, as well as feed the family on the above-average pub grub, including some good seafood, as well as enjoy the beer garden in summer.

The biggest event on the calendar for heavy lovers is undoubtedly the annual **Caledonian Beer Festival** (*✆ 0131 623 8066 for information*), a very popular event held at the start of June. Here you will find over 100 different beers from Britain and Ireland, including many types of heavy and also lagers. Entertainment and BBQ food is available in a carnival atmosphere.

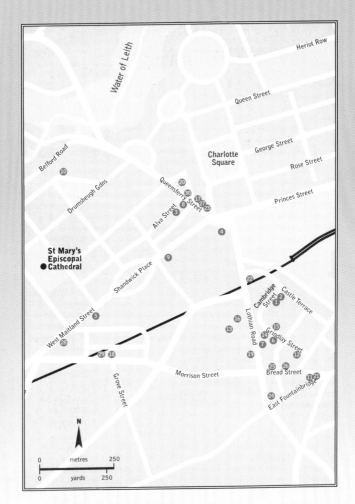

West End and Lothian Road

The business heart of Edinburgh's rapidly growing financial 'city' is based in the West End. Lothian Road was a rundown area even as recently as five years ago, but the new business developments have given the area a much needed shot in the arm and led to a renaissance both on Lothian Road and on the surrounding streets.

WEST END AND LOTHIAN ROAD
Restaurants

Atrium ❶

10 Cambridge St

✆ 0131 228 8882

🚌 Bus 1, 10, 11, 15, 16

Open: Mon–Fri 1200–1400, 1830–2200, Sat 1830–2200, closed Sun

Reservations essential

All credit cards accepted

Scottish

💷💷💷

With top Scots chef Andrew Radford at the helm, this classy restaurant is still going strong despite recent attempts amongst some of the local press to knock him down. Moody, dark décor works if you are seated facing away from the windows, but is not so impressive if you are facing out on to the theatre forecourt. Impressive, though, is the food, with fresh seafood and meat given the Radford treatment and desserts, including the legendary sticky toffee pudding, to die for.

blue bar café ❷

10 Cambridge St

✆ 0131 221 1222

🚌 Bus 1, 10, 11, 15, 16

Open: Mon–Fri 1200–1445, 1800–2245, Sat 1200–1445, 1800–0100, Sun 1200–1400

Reservations recommended

All credit cards accepted

Scottish/French

💷💷

Andrew Radford is also behind this more informal accompaniment to the Atrium. The ambience is bright and breezy with an array of Mediterranean delights. Choose from *focaccia* and cured Italian meat starters through to mains of the likes of seared salmon and wild mushroom ravioli.

Bouzy Rouge ❸

1A Alva St

✆ 0131 225 9594

🚌 Bus 40, 41, 41A

Open: Sun–Thu 1200–2130, Fri–Sat 1200–2230

Reservations recommended

All credit cards accepted

Scottish

💷💷

Nothing French about this basement restaurant apart from the name. A Glaswegian-run venture that offers quality cuisine in unstuffy surrounds. The décor is modern without that tinge of soulessness that can accompany some trendy restaurants.

Chisholm's ❹

Caledonian Hilton Hotel, Princes St

☏ 0131 459 9988
🚌 Bus 1, 10, 11, 15, 16
Open: daily, 1230–1430,
1800–2300

Reservations recommended

All credit cards accepted

Scottish

💷💷

New restaurant set in the old railway station that forms part of the city's foremost luxury hotel. Atmospheric surroundings with the old red-stone station façade the backdrop to light and creative cuisine. Good service and a decent wine list make it the perfect venue for a lazy lunch or an early dinner.

Indian Cavalry Club ⑤

3 Atholl Pl

☏ 0131 228 3282

🚌 Bus 1, 10, 11, 15, 16

Open: daily, 1200–1430, 1730–2400

Reservations recommended

All credit cards accepted

Jacket and tie recommended

Indian

💷💷

This is one of Edinburgh's classier Indian venues with excellent service and pleasing décor adding to the culinary experience. A restaurant regarded by many locals as the city's best Indian. Choose to dine in either the Club Tent or the Officer's Mess.

Jasmines ⑥

32 Grindlay St

☏ 0131 229 5757

🚌 Bus 1, 10, 11, 15, 16

Open: Mon–Thu 1100–2230, Fri 1200–1400, 1700–0030, Sat 1400–0030, Sun 1400–2330

Reservations recommended

💳 🔵 American Express

Chinese

💷

Edinburgh has many tacky Chinese restaurants where the décor looks like a Chinese B-movie film set, but thankfully this is not one of them. In this bright modern space you can enjoy well-prepared Chinese food, excellent steamed *dim sum* at any time of day and banquet menus.

Lazio ⑦

95 Lothian Rd

☏ 0131 229 7788

🚌 Bus 1, 10, 11, 15, 16

Open: Mon–Thu 1700–0130, Fri–Sat 1200–0300, Sun 1200–0130

Reservations recommended

💳 🔵 American Express

Italian

💷

Late-opening Italian that buzzes with the energy of many real Italian restaurants. On offer is a great range of pasta, pizza and meat dishes, as well as the more unusual 'treat' of tripe, definitely an acquired taste, but its success should not really surprise in a country whose national dish is served inside a sheep stomach.

New Edinburgh Rendezvous ⑧

10A Queensferry St

☏ 0131 225 2023

🚌 Bus 40, 41, 41A

Open: Mon–Sat 1200–1400, 1730–2300, Sun 1300–2300

Reservations recommended

All credit cards accepted

Chinese

💷

It may be looking a bit shabby, but this is the original and still one of the best Chinese restaurants in town. Few surprises on the menu with the spicier regional nuances left out to concentrate on the standards that they do well. The crispy Peking duck is above average and a favourite with local businessmen. The wine list is a bit suspect so a better option is to stick to the food and the Chinese beers.

La Piazza ⑨

97–99 Shandwick Pl

☏ 0131 221 1150

🚌 Bus 1, 10, 11, 15, 16

Open: Mon–Sat 1200–2330, Sun 1700–2330

Reservations recommended

💳 🔵 American Express

Italian

💷

Bright business-like Italian with little time for all the usual trappings of Italian restaurants. Unfussy décor and quick service, coupled with well-cooked pasta and first-class pizzas, make this a great venue for a quick meal at any time of the day.

Restaurant at the Bonham

35 Drumsheugh Gdns

✆ 0131 226 6050

🚍 Bus 13, 19, 19A, 40, 41, 41A

Open: Sun–Thu 1200–1430, 1830–2130, Fri–Sat 1200–1430, 1830–2200

Reservations recommended

All credit cards accepted

Fusion

€€

Set in one of Edinburgh's most attractive modern hotels, the food tastes as good as the restaurant looks. Californian cuisine meets Scottish in a modernist space where dining out is a real experience. The much-hyped décor is indeed as good as the fresh, innovative food. Good value for such excellent quality and also a decent wine list.

Restaurant at the Point Hotel ⑪

34 Bread St

✆ 0131 221 5555

🚍 Bus 1, 10, 11, 15, 16

Open: Mon–Sat 1200–1400, 1800–2130, closed Sun

Reservations recommended

💳 American Express

Modern Scottish

€

One of the best deals in town with Scots cuisine served up in minimalist surroundings. The hotel itself has won many accolades for its impressive modern design,

with pop stars Oasis and Moby amongst recent guests. The menu takes Scottish mainstays and turns them on their heads, with an intriguing starter of haggis wrapped with filo pastry in a butter sauce.

Stac Polly ⑫

8–10 Grindlay St

✆ 0800 458 6058

🚍 Bus 1, 10, 11, 15, 16

Open: Mon–Fri 1200–1430, 1800–2300, Sat–Sun 1800–2300

Reservations essential

All credit cards accepted

Scottish

€€

Named after a Highland mountain, this is one of Edinburgh's most renowned restaurants. The somewhat tacky tartan décor may clash with the innovative food, but the whole thing works well. Also boasts the most famous starter in town – the by now legendary haggis in filo pastry with plum and coriander sauce. This innovation has been much copied, but this is still the best haggis starter around. Stac Polly was recently voted by *GQ* magazine as one of the best restaurants in Britain.

The Terrace ⑬

Sheraton Hotel, Lothian Rd

☎ 0131 229 9131

🚍 Bus 1, 10, 11, 15, 16

Open: daily, 1200–1400, 1800–2300

Reservations recommended

All credit cards accepted

International

❷❸

The best hotel buffet in the city. Here you can watch the happenings on Festival Square with a view of the castle as a backdrop. This is the perfect chance to sample such Scottish mainstays as smoked salmon and steak, as well as head further east with the made-to-order stir-frys. Great value if you are feeling hungry and the short cut to sampling a lot of different dishes if your time is limited.

Thai Orchid ⑭

44 Grindlay St

☎ 0131 228 4438

🚍 Bus 1, 10, 11, 15, 16

Open: Mon–Fri 1200–1430, 1730–2400, Sat–Sun 1730–2400

Reservations recommended

🏧 American Express

Thai

❸

Cosy restaurant just off Lothian Road serving above-average Thai cuisine. The décor is simple and the food is well presented with the spicy red curries and extensive vegetarian options the highlights.

Tuscan Square ⑮

30 Grindlay St

☎ 0131 221 9728

🚍 Bus 1, 10, 11, 15, 16

Open: Tue–Sat 1200–1430, 1730–2200

Reservations recommended

🏧 American Express

Mediterranean

❷❸

Part of the Royal Lyceum Theatre, this Mediterranean eatery is a classy affair. There is a restaurant upstairs for more formal meals, while a café/bar arrangement downstairs offers a choice of dining options.

▲ Tuscan Square

WEST END AND LOTHIAN ROAD
Bars, cafés and pubs

All Bar One

Exchange Plaza, 50 Lothian Rd

Bus 1, 10, 11, 15, 16

Open: Mon–Thu 1130–2400, Fri–Sat 1130–0100, Sun 1230–2300

A branch of the very popular nationwide chain that nestles right at Edinburgh's business heart. Pine tables and polished wooden floors create a mellow ambience with the food suitably informal. Modern British is the theme, with meals cooked with a minimum of fuss.

Bar Roma ⑰

39A Queensferry St

Bus 13, 19, 19A, 40, 41, 41A

Open: Sun–Thu 1200–2400, Fri–Sat 1200–0100

Big restaurant/bar that still manages to produce the goods, that is, if you want sturdy pasta dishes and a wide variety of pizzas. Beware the big groups who sometimes over-power, but if you are in a large group yourself this is one of the best places in town to come for a decent Italian meal. Child-friendly.

Cuba Norte ⑱

192 Morrison St

Bus 1, 10, 11, 15, 16

Open: Sun–Wed 1100–2400, Thu–Sat 1100–0100

One of Edinburgh's growing number of Cuban theme bars that specialise in Cuban cooking Miami-exile style. Good range of *tapas* that are somewhat bizarrely named after various types of cigars.

Filmhouse Café

88 Lothian Rd

Bus 1, 10, 11, 15, 16

Open: Sun–Thu 1000–2330, Fri–Sat 1000–0030

Mellow café/bar in Edinburgh's premier arthouse cinema. Choose from a surprisingly decent choice of main dishes, as well as cakes, before catching one of the excellent value afternoon matinees. Pop in even if you are not watching a

▲ Indigo Yard

movie to experience the arty buzz.

Indigo Yard  ⑳

7 Charlotte La

🚌 Bus 13, 19, 19A, 40, 41, 41A

Open: daily, 0830–0100

Painfully hip bar/café frequented by Edinburgh's *cognoscenti*. The courtyard area downstairs is very busy with people enjoying after-dinner drinks. The food can loosely be described as fusion with Mexican and North African slipping into the Pacific Rim mix.

Monboddo ㉑

34 Bread St

🚌 Bus 1, 10, 11, 15, 16

Open: Mon–Thu 1000–2400, Fri–Sat 1000–0100, Sun 1100–2400

The very trendy bar at the equally trendy Point Hotel. A bright, modern space with plenty of black leather and sharp edges. A see-and-be-seen place, perfect for a light lunch or drinks and a snack. Great range of tempting cocktail concoctions on offer.

Muse Bar ㉒

21 Lothian Rd

🚌 Bus 1, 10, 11, 15, 16

Open: daily, 1100–0100

A new bar just across from Edinburgh's rapidly growing financial centre. Here you will find a fully stocked bar, as well as a fairly extensive lunch menu to cater for the office workers across the road. Propping up the menu is a basic range of sandwiches and baked potatoes, as well as heartier lasagne and fish and chips.

Ryans ㉓

2–4 Hope St

🚌 Bus 1, 10, 11, 15, 16

Open: Mon–Wed 1200–2300, Thu 1200–2400, Fri–Sat 1200–0100, Sun 1800–2300

Great location with huge windows at the end of Princes Street. Has a reputation as being the exclusive preserve of the besuited nine-to-five office crowd, but actually attracts a diverse clientele. Delve below street level to the bistro downstairs and discover a lively kitchen that dishes up French standards in cosy surroundings.

Uluru ㉔

133 Lothian Rd

🚌 Bus 1, 10, 11, 15, 16

Open: Mon–Thu 1100–2400, Fri–Sat 1100–0100, Sun 1600–2400

Named after the world's most famous rock (Ayers Rock) in Australia, this loosely themed Australian café/bar is a popular lunch and snack spot on Lothian Road. The décor follows its namesake with ochre and warm red hues, while the food skirts around the Mediterranean as well as cosmopolitan Sydney.

Web 13 ㉕

13 Bread St

🚌 Bus 1, 10, 11, 15, 16

Open: Mon–Fri 0900–2200, Sat 0900–2200, Sun 0900–2200

An internet café that buzzes with life and filling food. Surf at some of the city's cheapest rates as you munch on huge breakfast *panini* melts and all-day breakfasts. Also more healthy salads and tortilla wraps. As popular with office workers popping in for a takeaway lunch as it is amongst the net surfers who flock here. The friendly staff are equally happy sorting out your sandwich as they are your PC.

WEST END AND LOTHIAN ROAD
Shops, markets and picnic sites

Shops

Bread Street Deli 26

27 Bread Street

◉ Bus 1, 10, 11, 15, 16

Open: Mon–Sat 0830–2100,
Sun 1030–1900

Wonderful food shop in
an unlikely location,
just off busy Lothian
Road. Homemade pâtés,
houmous and spices
abound in an extensive
range. It also boasts a
huge cheese counter
and a meat counter
with a selection of
Italian and Spanish
cooked meats.

Carrs 27

41 Queensferry St

◉ Bus 40, 41, 41A

Open: Mon–Fri 0715–1800,
Sat 0815–1600, closed Sun

Carrs is one of the best
grocers in this part of

▲ Bread Street Deli

town. They stock a
decent range of fresh
fruit and vegetables.
They also have a sepa-
rate cheese and cooked
meat counter and sell
pre-cooked vegetarian
meals made by
Hendersons.

Le Marché Français 28

9A West Maitland St

◉ First Bus 16, 17, 18

Open: Mon–Sat 0730–2100,
closed Sun

Demonstrating the
strength of the 'Auld
Alliance' between
Scotland and France,
this fantastic new shop
specialises in everything
French. It only opened a
month before the new
millennium, but it has
quickly established a
dedicated following
with a first-class range
of cheese and wines
from over the Channel.
Pop in for a cheese or
wine sample and be
transformed to France.

Special Scotch Whisky 29

224 Morrison St

◉ Bus 1, 10, 11, 15, 16

Open: Mon–Sat 0900–1700,
closed Sun

A great selection of
unusual whiskies is

▲ Le Marché Français

found in this small shop,
which deals in the often
rare grain whiskies –
but, beware, they are not
always in stock. Teas
and preserves are also
sold, as well as stylish
decanters, glasses and
whisky miniatures.
A real whisky lover's
paradise.

Welch's Quality Fish 30

39 Queensferry St

◉ Bus 40, 41, 41A

Open: Mon–Fri 0800–1730,
Sat 0800–1700, closed Sun

One of the city's best
fishmongers. Here you
will find all the most
popular types of fresh
fish, including salmon,
Arbroath Smokies and
the ubiquitous haddock.
They also sell mussels
and frozen fish. Even if
you do not intend to
buy anything, it is
worth popping into one
of the city's fishmon-
ger's just to get an idea
of the richness of
Scotland's seafood.

Literary pubs

The loosening of tongues

Like its Celtic twin, Dublin, across the Irish Sea, Edinburgh is a city whose literary heritage is intrinsically bound up with its pubs. In Edinburgh's nefarious drinking dens many great creative minds have been inspired, corrupted or deadened by an endless stream of ale and whisky. From the days of Robert Burns (Scotland's national poet) right through to more recent literary luminaries such as Irvine Welsh (*Trainspotting* and *Acid House*), the Edinburgh literati have pounded the cobbled streets in search of the inspiration that they frequently found in its pubs.

To travel back through the centuries, head for the **White**

Heart Inn (*34 The Grassmarket*). As you sup your drink look around and imagine three centuries ago when the young Ayrshire poet Robert Burns, author of *Auld Lang Syne* and countless better poems and songs, came to the city and penned *Ae Fond Kiss*.

One of Edinburgh's greatest literary sons was Robert Louis Stevenson. Although one of his most famous novels, *The Mysterious Case of Dr Jekyll and Mr Hyde*, was supposed to be set in London, few doubt that the tight wynds and narrow streets of the novel are meant to represent Edinburgh and that he was trying only thinly to veil his attack on some of his enemies in the city.

This theory is given further weight by the mysterious case of Deacon Brodie, a respected local citizen who was eventually revealed as a criminal and hanged in the Grassmarket on gallows that, ironically, he had helped to design. This duality between rationality and respectability on the one side and the more sinister, wilder side of human nature on the other is a recurrent theme in Edinburgh and was the central focus of Stevenson's novel. Today you can ponder which city he was really writing about when you drop inside **Deacon Brodie's Tavern** (*435 Lawnmarket, Royal Mile*). Good pub lunches are on offer downstairs, with more formal meals upstairs.

The Stevenson theme continues down in the New Town at the **Jekyll and Hyde** (*112 Hanover St*). This theme bar offers decent pub grub and a good range of drinks. Bizarrely, the toilet is the highlight: the entrance door is disguised as a bookshelf and half the fun is watching bemused drinkers trying to stumble through the right door.

Further out of Edinburgh you can delve even deeper into Stevenson's work at the **Hawes Inn** (*7 Newhalls Rd, South Queensferry; ✆ 0131 319 1120; ◉ train to Dalmeny from Waverley Station; ✆ 08705 484950 for times and prices*). It was in this atmospheric old tavern that Stevenson penned much of his novel, *Kidnapped*, with the pub itself featuring as the title and content of a whole chapter. For Stevenson buffs this is an unmissable attraction. For those unfamiliar with his work, come here just to feast on the good pub food, including chicken stuffed with haggis, and spend a night in one of the upstairs rooms that overlook the Firth of Forth.

At the rougher end of the literary experience is **Rutherglens** (*Drummond St*). There are rumours that both Arthur Conan Doyle and Stevenson drank here when they were students. The pub was always a rough and ready affair and that has not

changed today, so if you want to visit, dress down and prepare to sample a real taste of working-class Scottish life.

A far more salubrious experience is on offer at **Greyfriars Bobby** (*24 Candlemaker Row*). This old pub is named after the famous dog who devoted himself to a tramp that he had befriended. When the tramp died the dog spent the rest of his own life lying by his master's grave. Basic pub grub is on offer in the bar. A small statue across the road depicts the dog and the Greyfriars graveyard itself is a short stroll away.

For a fuller picture of the rich literary life of the city, take one of the pub tours (*The Scottish Literary Tour Company; all year round; ✆ 0131 226 6665 for times of tours*) that start from the **Beehive Inn** (*The Grassmarket*). You will be led along the Old Town's atmospheric streets by two actors, who will recite the works of the city's literary finest, and visit pubs with literary connections.

> **In Edinburgh's nefarious drinking dens many great creative minds have been inspired, corrupted or deadened by an endless stream of ale and wine.**

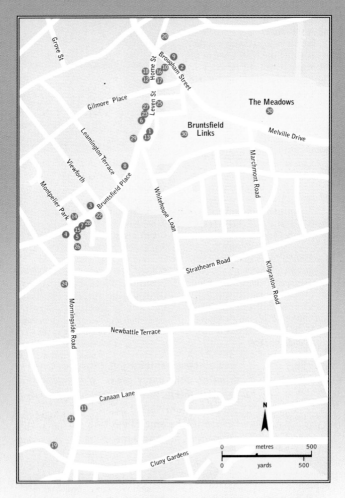

Tollcross, Bruntsfield and Morningside

Edinburgh's main upper-class enclave, Morningside, likes to see itself as a cut above the rest of the city and is laden with niche market food shops. Neighbouring Bruntsfield is catching up fast and once down-trodden Tollcross is in the middle of a massive regeneration that has brought a sweep of new eateries to the Home Street area.

TOLLCROSS, BRUNTSFIELD AND MORNINGSIDE
Restaurants

The Apartment ❶

7–13 Barclay Pl

✆ 0131 228 6456

🚍 Bus 11, 15, 16

Open: Sun–Fri 1800–2300,
Sat 1200–1500, 1800–
2300

Reservations essential

VISA 💳 American Express

Fusion

❻❻

Stylish new eatery that
packs in a youngish
crowd of locals. The
ambience is of a
Guggenheim-style art
gallery with stark pine
tables and sharp lines.
The service is very

relaxed, as is the
atmosphere. Expect
innovative fusion style
cuisine that you can
share *tapas* style with
your dining compan-
ions. Good value, even if
you end up embroiled in
one of oddball hands-on
owner Malcolm Innes'
spiralling conversations.

Bombay Bicycle Club ❷

6–6A Brougham Pl

✆ 0131 229 3839

🚍 Bus 1, 10, 11, 15, 16

Open: daily, 1200–1400,
1730–2400

Reservations recommended

VISA 💳 American Express

Indian

❻

Based on the Bombay
original, this eatery is
split into two sections.
At the front is a more
informal, light room
and a longer, more inti-
mate space at the back.
Bengali cuisine rules
with good priced set
menus and decent
vegetarian options.

Giardino D'Italia ❸

158 Bruntsfield Pl

✆ 0131 229 3325

🚍 Bus 11, 15, 16

Open: Tue–Sat 1200–1500,
1700–2400, Sun–Mon
1700–2300

Reservations recommended

American Express

Italian

This restaurant is more
Sicilian than many in
Palermo and the food
rarely disappoints. The
décor may veer on the
tacky side, especially
the plastic plants, but
the food saves the day.
If you thought Italian
food was never spicy, be
prepared to set your
tastebuds alight with
chilli, garlic and ginger
spicing up many of the
dishes.

Howie's

208 Bruntsfield Pl

☎ 0131 221 1777

🚌 Bus 11, 15, 16

Open: daily, 1200–1430,
1800–2200

Reservations recommended

American Express

Scottish

One of the group of
three Howie's restau-
rants that have consis-
tently performed on the
Edinburgh restaurant
scene for over a decade.
Howie's holds a special
place in the hearts of
most locals and it's easy
to see why. Good, solid
Scottish raw materials
such as salmon and
black pudding are on
offer, all laced with
interesting sauces. The
atmosphere shies away
from too much formality
and the BYOB drink

policy makes a visit to
Howie's a relaxing
restaurant experience.

Inca

183 Bruntsfield Pl

☎ 0131 228 4555

🚌 Bus 11, 15, 16

Open: daily, 1100–0100

Reservations recommended

American Express

Mediterranean

Everyone will feel at
home at this friendly
neighbourhood bistro.
Pop in for a coffee and
leaf through the daily
papers or come for a
full meal in a very
homely atmosphere that
defies you not to relax.
The portions are huge
and good value with a
favouritism for all
things Italian. Children
welcome.

Jacques

8 Gillespie Pl

☎ 0131 229 6080

🚌 Bus 11, 15, 16

Open: Mon–Sat 1200–1430,
1730–2230, closed Sun

Reservations recommended

American Express

French/Scottish

Scottish and French
cuisine may seem
unlikely bedfellows, but
the 'Auld Alliance'
works well on this
occasion. The freshness
of the crossover menu is
demonstrated by the
fact that it changes
greatly, depending on
the season. An intimate,
candlelit bistro-style

restaurant with few
tourists and always a
friendly welcome.

Montpeliers

159–161 Bruntsfield Pl

☎ 0131 229 3115

🚌 Bus 11, 15, 16

Open: daily, 0900–0100

Reservations recommended

American Express

Mediterranean

Transformed completely
from its former guise as
a dingy old pub, this is
now one of the best
bar-style restaurants in
Edinburgh. The feel is
cosmopolitan chic with
Mediterranean-style
food, huge salads and a
wide range of drinks.
In summer the
Mediterranean theme
continues as they open
the windows and let the
tables spill on to the
street outside. A great
choice for a warm day
or a lazy Sunday lunch.

The Potting
Shed

69 Bruntsfield Pl

☎ 0131 229 1393

🚌 Bus 11, 15, 16

Open: Mon–Fri 1730–2130,
Sat 1200–1400, 1730–
2130, Sun 1200–1400,
1730–2130

Reservations recommended

All credit cards accepted

Scottish

A quality Scottish
restaurant that hides in
a candlelit conservatory
below the Best Western-
owned Bruntsfield

Hotel. Traditional Scots specialities are updated and served in elegant and comfortable surroundings. One of the classiest venues in this part of town.

Shamiana  ⑨

14 Brougham St
✆ 0131 228 2265
🚍 Bus 1, 10, 11, 15, 16
Open: Mon–Thu 1830–2200, Fri–Sat 1830–2230, Sun 1830–2100
Reservations essential
All credit cards accepted
Indian
ⓖ ⓔ

This is just about as good as it gets when it comes to Indian restaurants in Edinburgh. If it is good enough for celebrities and politicians such as Gordon Brown, then it is good enough for the locals and they flock here religiously to feast on the northern Indian cuisine. The chief chef recently won the Best Chef Award in the revered *Good Curry Guide*, an achievement recreated every night in this restaurant.

Sukothai ⑩

23 Brougham Pl
✆ 0131 229 1537
🚍 Bus 1, 10, 11, 15, 16
Open: daily, 1200–1430, 1730–2230
Reservations recommended
💳 American Express
Thai
ⓖ

A busy ethnic eatery that offers a slice of

▲ Montpeliers

Thailand right at the centre of rapidly changing Tollcross. No pretensions here as all of the main Thai dishes are served up with the minimum of fuss. The highlight is the excellent range of noodle dishes and vegetarian options; Sunday lunches are especially good value.

TOLLCROSS, BRUNTSFIELD AND MORNINGSIDE
Bars, cafés and pubs

Cannymans ⑪

239 Morningside Rd

⊙ Bus 11, 15, 16

Open: Mon–Wed 1200–2300, Thu 1200–2400, Fri 1200–0100, Sat 1200–2400, Sun 1230–2330

Some say it is too intimidating, but a visit here is an unforgettable experience. The walls are bedecked with all sorts of bric-à-brac, the staff are spitefully surly and huge signs declare that you can't take any photos of that stunning film set-like interior. The smorgasbord lunches, though, are worth braving the staff for – just keep that camera safely tucked away.

Fifila ⑫

60 Home St

⊙ Bus 11, 15, 16

Open: daily, 1100–2200

Bright little café with delights from all over the world. One day when you go in it appears to be mainly a takeaway and the next a sit-down café. Take your pick and choose the spicy wraps for a walk on Home Street or laze through something more substantial at their cosy pine tables.

Golf Tavern ⑬

31 Wright's Houses

⊙ Bus 11, 15, 16

Open: Mon–Thu 1200–2400, Fri–Sat 1200–0100, Sun 1230–2400

Overlooking Bruntsfield Links, this pub feels as though it has been flown in from the countryside. The golf course is a tiny pitch and putt affair, but the atmosphere inside the popular Golf Tavern is warm

and friendly. Ask at the bar for a free game of golf. Traditional pub grub is the order of the day, with cajun sausage and mash, and beef and ale pies perennial favourites.

Le Grand Cafetière ⑭

182–184 Bruntsfield Pl

⊙ Bus 11, 15, 16

Open: Mon–Wed 0900–2300, Thu–Sat 0900–2400, Sun 1000–1800

A surprisingly eclectic eatery tucked away in Bruntsfield. Choose from a wide array of dishes, everything from baguettes and big breakfasts through to light sandwiches and muffins. Families welcome during the day, with a special children's menu, but at night things take on a more formal air with more substantial main dishes.

Grinders Coffee Co. ⑮

165A Bruntsfield Pl

⊙ Bus 11, 15, 16

Open: Mon–Thu 0800–1900, Fri–Sat 0800–1800, Sun 1000–1700

Replaces the short-lived Mango and Stone juice bar, which didn't quite fit in with Edinburgh's

climate. Grinders opened in January 2000, specialising in a range of coffees and well-filled bagels, but it also plans to branch out into Mango and Stone territory and try a limited range of fruit juices.

Ndelbe 16

57 Home St

🚌 Bus 11, 15, 16

Open: daily, 1000–2200

The place in town for homesick South Africans. Here you will find South African confectionery and groceries, alongside some excellent themed food. The *mielie mielie* bread is the best this side of Cape Town and the *boerewors* sausage is perfectly spiced. Chose from the street-level café where you can watch local life drift by or the basement where you can hide away.

Piemaker 17

64 Home St

🚌 Bus 11, 15, 16

Open: Mon–Thu 0900–2000, Fri 0900–2300, Sat 1000–2300, Sun 1100–1900

If you like pies then you will be in heaven in Piemaker. This small outlet buzzes all day long with locals and tourists alike flocking to feast on the eclectic range of pies, everything from perennial favourites such as cheese, spinach, and chicken with mushroom, right through to spicy vegetable bajan and

maple with pecan. They also sell frozen pies if you prefer to cook them for yourself.

Rialto 18

37 Home St

🚌 Bus 11, 15, 16

Open: daily, 1000–2400

Very good value new café/bar. Here you will find a strange mixture of Italian and Scottish fare with pizzas and pasta dishes on the one side and sturdy mains like haddock on the other. It also does a very cheap set lunch menu.

Waiting Room 19

7 Belhaven Terrace

🚌 Bus 11, 15, 16

Open: daily, 1000–2000

Railway-themed informal bistro laden with railway touches such as carriage-shaped windows and suitcases in luggage racks. A range of pub-style grub with burgers and cooked breakfasts is complemented by more adventurous main dishes.

Where To? 20

103 High Riggs, Tollcross

🚌 Bus 1, 10, 11, 15, 16

Open: daily, 0800–2200

Calling it an internet café would not be doing this bright café justice. Here you can surf the web, order snacks or even enjoy a full meal. A perfect place to relax and catch up with your e-mails.

TOLLCROSS, BRUNTSFIELD AND MORNINGSIDE
Shops, markets and picnic sites

Shops

W & S Dickson ㉑

326 Morningside Rd

◉ Bus 11, 15, 16

Open: Mon–Sat 0800–1730, closed Sun

Basic grocer amongst the fine food shops in this part of town. Stocks a range of fresh fruit and vegetables, as well as such interesting items as farmhouse biscuits.

The Engine Shed ㉒

123 Bruntsfield Pl

◉ Bus 11, 15, 16

Open: Mon–Sat 1000–1715, closed Sun

Simple food shop with a conscience that trains people with learning difficulties to work in the shop and behind the scenes. Limited range of cakes, olive oils, organic produce and breads with a health-food theme.

Global Fruits ㉓

5 Gillespie Pl

◉ Bus 11, 15, 16

Open: Mon–Sat 0700–1900, Sun 0900–1800

Eclectic food shop selling a good range of items, including pak choi, lemon grass and plum tomatoes. Always busy with locals stocking up on those diverse items that are often so difficult to find in Edinburgh.

Gourmet Pasta ㉔

54–56 Morningside Rd

◉ Bus 11, 15, 16

Open: daily, 1000–1800

They do make their own pasta, but they also bake their own filo pastries, pizzas and a variety of other goodies, including olives, peppers, quiche, cooked meats, as well as more sugary treats such as tiramisu. They also stock Brodies coffee, which is roasted down in Leith.

Lupe Pinto's Deli ㉕

24 Leven St

◉ Bus 11, 15, 16

Open: Mon–Sat 1000–1800, closed Sun

Fantastic deli specialising in Mexican, Spanish and Italian produce. Such is the quality of the Spanish produce that Lupe Pinto's supplies many of the city's Spanish-themed cafés and bars. This is the place in town to grab some *chorizo* or *jamón serrano*, on the advice, of course, of its knowledgeable staff. A good range of international wines and beers is also stocked.

Ian Mellis ㉖

205 Bruntsfield Pl

◉ Bus 11, 15, 16

Open: Mon–Wed 0930–1830, Thu 0930–1700, Fri 0930–1830, Sat 0900–1800, Sun 1000–1700

Fantastic shop that sells Mellis's speciality cheeses. The range is more international, though, than the Victoria Street branch (*see page 24*) with other international goodies such as *chorizo*, *jamón serrano* and butter 'the way they used to make it' all on sale. One of the best places in town to put together an unforgettable picnic or just to rummage around, soaking in the aromas and enjoying the tasty samples dished out by the friendly staff.

Neptunes ㉗

23 Leven St

🚌 Bus 11, 15, 16

Open: Tue–Fri, Sun 0730–1730, Sat 0730–1700, closed Mon

Great range of fresh fish served up with a hearty smile by the real characters who work here. All the staples are here, including haddock, salmon and trout, along with some frozen specials such as mussels and oysters.

Peckhams ㉘

155–159 Bruntsfield Pl

🚌 Bus 11, 15, 16

Open: Mon–Sat 0800–2400, Sun 0900–2400

One of Edinburgh's best food shops located right next to the Meadows. Freshness guaranteed, with plump olives, dips, cheeses and cooked meats making up impressive displays. Extensive range of

▲ Ian Mellis

Macsweens haggis and a range of international beers. A downstairs café in the Valvona and Crolla style was added in February 2000.

Scott's Deli ㉙

1 Gillespie Cres

🚌 Bus 11, 15, 16

Open: Mon–Sat 1000–1800, Sun 1200–1600

Fantastic food shop with three rooms. The first sells a fine range of fresh foods, baking and sandwiches. The second is an eclectic grocer and the third has refrigerated items, including the legendary Mrs Unis naan breads (which she supplies to many of Edinburgh's restaurants). Good place to buy food for a picnic on Bruntsfield Links.

Picnic sites

The Meadows/ Bruntsfield Links ㉚

🚌 Bus 11, 15, 16

Open: all day

Expansive city-centre parks that offer great views out across towards the dormant Arthur's Seat volcano. Very much a lived-in space with students lazing on the benches, impromptu games of football in summer, tennis courts and a children's playground. Head for one of Bruntsfield's great delis, put together a picnic, and join in the fun out on the grass.

Vegetarian restaurants

A blossoming trend

Ten years ago you would have been hard pushed to find more than a couple of acceptable vegetarian restaurants in a city where 'meat and two veg' was as near as most people got to vegetarianism. Thankfully times have changed and Edinburgh now has a good choice of vegetarian options, everything from informal takeaway-style outlets through to more formal venues for dinner. And such is the quality of many that they are now popular with committed carnivores looking for the occasional healthier option.

> **Culinary miracles are performed with inventive dishes that bring gourmet cooking to vegetarian cuisine.**

Edinburgh as a whole is far more considerate towards vegetarian diners than many places in mainland Europe. Chefs no longer lift the meat out of a dish and then serve it up as a vegetarian meal as can often still happen in some European countries. In most city restaurants there are usually a few choices for vegetarian starters and mains, and even in many of the city's pubs the basic bar menu features at least one vegetarian option.

One of the city's best-known vegetarian restaurants is **Henderson's** (*94 Hanover St; ✆ 0131 225 2131; open: Mon–Sat 0800–2230; closed Sun;* ❸❸).

This is reputed to be Scotland's oldest vegetarian restaurant, dating back some 35 years. This friendly self-service eatery is also very versatile in that you will feel equally comfortable coming in for a light breakfast, feasting on the set lunch menus or coming along for a full-blown dinner.

Just around the corner from Henderson's is the oft-neglected **Henderson's Bistro** (*25 Thistle St; ✆ 0131 225 2605; open: Mon–Tue 1200–1500, Wed 1145–1900, Thu–Sat 1200–2230, Sun 1200–1800;* ❸❸), which allows you the luxury of table service with not that large a step up in price. It is a good place if you want a cosy meal or a venue that feels like a real restaurant experience rather than just a relaxed eatery for vegetarians.

Bann's (*5 Hunter Sq; ✆ 0131 226 1112; open: daily 1000–2300;* ❸), an oasis tucked just off the Royal Mile, is another relaxed vegetarian eatery. The small interior is always busy with a mix of locals and tourists and in summer there are outdoor tables. By day the atmosphere is very informal, though at night out come the tablecloths and snappier service. Bann's manages to steer way clear of the blander vegetarian staples and spice things up with influences from Mexico and the Pacific Rim.

Black Bo's (*57–61 Blackfriars St; ✆ 0131 557 6136; open: Mon–Sat 1200–1400, 1800–2230, Sun 1800–2230;* ❷❷) is a step up in class from these eateries and is also home to its legendary vegetarian haggis. In this moody space culinary miracles are performed with inventive dishes that bring gourmet cooking to vegetarian cuisine. The famed vegetarian haggis justifies the hype and will please both vegetarians and meat eaters who are not brave enough to try the original.

▲ Henderson's

Kalpna (*2–3 St Patrick's Sq; ✆ 0131 667 9890; open: Sun–Fri 1200–1400, 1730–2300, Sat 1730–2300;* ❷) is not only a great vegetarian restaurant, but also one of the best Indian restaurants in the city. This Edinburgh institution has been going strong for a decade and a half with no sign of letting standards slip. Even the most dedicated carnivore will struggle to resist its excellent curries and spicier dishes with ingredients sourced all the way from India.

Another vegetarian restaurant that takes its cues from the subcontinent is **Ann Purna** (*45 St. Patrick's Sq; ✆ 0131 662 1807; open: Mon–Fri 1200–1400, 1730–2300, Sat–Sun 1730–2300;* ❷). This vegetarian and vegan restaurant is just a short stroll away from Edinburgh University and, not surprisingly, fills up with students and their tutors. The décor is nothing startling, but the cooking is fresh and spicy with enough to tingle the palate for lunch or dinner.

If you are looking for a cosy café that offers vegetarian cooking then there is no better place in Edinburgh than **Isabel's Café** (*83 Clerk St; ✆ 0131 662 4014; open: Mon 1130–1530, Tue 1130–1530, Wed–Fri 1130–1530, Sat 1130–1530; closed Sun;* ❷), which is tucked below the popular **Nature's Gate** health-food shop (*see page 35*). The cooking may be homemade in style, but it is fairly inventive and seldom disappoints, with such staples as vegetarian ratatouille and apple pudding just like your Mum used to make it.

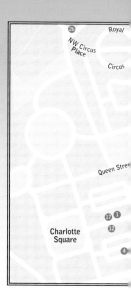

The New Town

The perfect symmetry of the grid-like New Town streets is laden with many eating and drinking opportunities. The choice is diverse, with Rose Street the best venue for pub grub while George Street is moving continually upmarket with a number of bank to bar/restaurant conversions and some classy eateries catering for the local business community.

THE NEW TOWN
Restaurants

Brown's ❶

131–133 George St

✆ 0131 225 4442

🚌 Bus 1, 10, 12, 15

Open: Mon–Sat 1100–0100, Sun 1200–0100

Reservations recommended

All credit cards accepted

British

💷💷

Brown's has several branches across Britain, this one in a surprisingly grand building in George Street. A voluminous ceiling, circling fans and leafy plants dotted around all give the impression of a bygone era. If you are in the mood for an unsophisticated meal in a sophisticated setting, this is the place to come.

Le Chambertin ❷

21 George St

✆ 0131 240 7178

🚌 Bus 13

Open: Tue–Fri 1230–1400, 1900–2200, Sat 1900–2200, closed Sun–Mon

Reservations recommended

All credit cards accepted

Jacket and tie required

Fri–Sat dinner

Scottish/French

💷💷

An elegant dining-room with polished service that nestles in the George Street Intercontinental Hotel. The cuisine veers on traditional despite a few attempts, such as the whisky-laced haggis starter, to infuse some new ideas. If you are looking for an up-market restaurant with a grand, regal feel, then

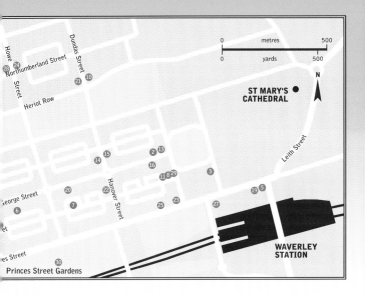

this is the place to head for.

Erewan Oriental

14 South St Andrew St
✆ 0131 556 4242
🚌 Bus 1, 10, 12, 15
Open: daily, 1200–1430, 1700–2300
Reservations recommended
💳 💳 American Express
Thai
£ £

An ethnic restaurant that manages not to fall into the trap of covering its walls with tacky kitsch. Instead, you really do feel as though you are in some turn-of-the-century colonial hotel in Bangkok. Very polished look and service. Excellent value lunch specials as well as banquets for two or three, which cut the cost while letting you try a bit of everything.

Get Stuffed 4

192 Rose St
✆ 0131 225 2208
🚌 Bus 1, 10, 12, 15
Open: Mon–Fri 1200–1400, 1800–2300, Sat 1730–2300, closed Sun
Reservations recommended
💳 💳
American
£ £

If you are hungry then this is definitely the right place. The limited menu is stuffed full of meat, meat and more meat. The specialities are huge burgers, which make a quick lunch before an afternoon of sightseeing or shopping back with the crowds on Princes Street. Get Stuffed is also renowned as having some of the biggest steaks in town, and serves Crombies' famous 'Auld Reekie' sausages.

Hadrian's 5

Balmoral Hotel, 1 Princes St
✆ 0131 557 5000
🚌 Bus 1, 10, 12, 15
Open: Mon–Sat 1200–1430, 1830–2230, Sun 1230–1500, 1830–2230
Reservations recommended

plucked from the ocean and it has. The two men behind the Mussel Inn are Scottish shellfish farmers who ensure that only the freshest ingredients are used. The décor is on the functional side and the side dishes are nothing special, but for fresh seafood in the New Town this is the place. The kilo pots of mussels, laced with various flavours and served with crusty bread, are a speciality.

Rhodes and Co

3 Rose St

✆ 0131 220 9190

🚍 Bus 1, 10, 12, 15

Open: Mon–Sat 1200–1430, 1830–2230, Sun 1200–1430

Reservations recommended

All credit cards accepted

British

💷💷

The latest regional outlet for superchef Gary Rhodes, this modern brasserie-style restaurant serves up delicious British cuisine. Appearing on the menu are earthy specials such as bacon and beans, haddock and chips and the delightful whisky rice pudding with fresh raspberries. Everything is spiced up with the typical Rhodes flair, though he only visits this Edinburgh branch occasionally and there has been some recent sniping over the use of frozen chips.

All credit cards accepted

Scottish

💷💷

Less formal and renowned than its sibling, No. 1, this restaurant is still up there with the city's best. Jeff Bland, the chef behind No. 1, infuses the menu with enough high-quality produce and innovative dishes to offer a serious alternative to the hotel's signature restaurant. The lunch menu specials are good value. Hadrian's also throws open its doors to non-residents for breakfast if you are staying somewhere more modest and want to sample a touch of the high life.

Martin's

70 Rose St North La

✆ 0131 225 3106

🚍 Bus 1, 10, 12, 15

Open: Tue–Fri 1200–1400, 1900–2200, Sat 1900–2200, closed Sun–Mon

Reservations recommended

All credit cards accepted

Scottish

💷💷

Pleasant restaurant hidden away from view just off the main section of Rose Street. The hand-written menu changes daily in a restaurant that has long been a favourite of Edinburgh's chattering classes.

Mussel Inn

61–65 Rose St

✆ 0131 225 5979

🚍 Bus 1, 10, 12, 15

Open: Mon–Fri 1200–1500, 1800–2200, Sat 1200–2200, Sun 1330–2200

Reservations recommended

All credit cards accepted

Seafood

💷

Seafood that tastes as though it has just been

Tippoo Sahib 🟉

129A Rose St

☎ 0131 226 2862

🚍 Bus 1, 10, 12, 15

Open: Mon–Sat 1200–1400, 1730–2330, Sun 1700–2330

Reservations recommended

All credit cards accepted

Indian

🟢

Strange décor depicts Scottish soldiers and their military endeavours in the subcontinent during the 18th century. The food itself is not nearly as bizarre, with all of the usual favourite curries watered down for the Scottish palate, but this is as good an Indian curry as you will get in this part of town.

Winter Glen 🟉

3 Dundas St

☎ 0131 477 7060

🚍 Bus 23

Open: Mon–Thu 1200–1400, 1800–2200, Fri–Sat 1200–1400, 1800–2230, closed Sun

Reservations essential

American Express

Scottish

🟢🟢

There is nothing desolate about this Winter Glen, which abounds with the best of Scots produce. There is no better place in Edinburgh for an Aberdeen Angus steak and the seafood and game dishes are also excellent.

THE NEW TOWN
Bars, cafés and pubs

The Abbottsford ⑪

3 Rose St

🚌 Bus 1, 10, 12, 15

Open: daily, 1200–2400

Authentic old-style bar with an informal eating area tucked above. The food is surprisingly good, steering away from normal pub fare towards Paris with mains such as Steak Diane. Also a decent wine list and a menu that rummages through Scotland's larder with haggis, steak and a heavenly cranachan dessert. One of the better pub lunch venues in Edinburgh.

Bar 38 ⑫

126–128 George St

🚌 Bus 13

Open: Mon–Sat 1000–0100, Sun 1000–2400

The bright, airy new bar opened in 1999, catering to tourists during the day and the office set in the evening. Backed by Scottish and Newcastle Brewers, it offers a wide range of drinks as well as sandwiches, salads and plates to share. There is a good brunch on Sundays and you can stoke up on full cooked breakfasts.

The Clans ⑬

21 George St

🚌 Bus 13

Open: daily, 1200–2400

Atmospheric Scottish bar set inside the George Intercontinental Hotel. Unlike many of the other bars in this increasingly buzzing street, this is a more sophisticated affair. Drinks are on the pricey side, as is the posh pub nosh, but the ambience must be experienced at least once.

Cyberia ⑭

88 Hanover St

🚌 Bus 23

Open: daily, 1000–2200

Expensive if you want to surf, but well worth going into to enjoy the funky décor and a good range of food. An alternative choice for lunch away from the Princes Street crowds, with baguettes and sandwiches as well as toasties with various fillings.

Dix Neuf ⑮

97 Hanover St

🚌 Bus 23

Open: daily, 0930–0100

Bright French brasserie where you are as equally at home launching into a three-course meal as you are

grabbing a coffee and croissant. Mellow piano accompaniment during the day changes to a guitar when the sun slips down and the menu does a similar sea change, with French breakfast staples giving way to more hearty evening meals that delve into French/ Scottish crossover territory.

The Dome

14 George St

Bus 13

Open: daily, 1200–late

WELCOME TO THE DOME

Probably the most impressive of Edinburgh's bank-to-bar conversions. The elegant interior oozes class and is usually busy with suits and tourists staring upwards and admiring the architecture, before settling down to the bistro-style cooking. For lunch, a good option is the club sandwich that beats most of the patchy efforts found in Edinburgh's hotels, while dinner sees the food head more towards the style of French–Scottish cuisine.

Est Est Est ⑰

145A George St

Bus 13

Open: daily, 1200–0100

Informal restaurant/bar that is almost always packed out with an eclectic mix of businessmen, families and tourists. Part of a larger chain, the food is not too exciting, but decent value for this part of town with the staples taking their cue from the Mediterranean.

MKB (Mykindabar) ⑱

45A North Castle Street

Bus 13

Open: Mon–Sat 1200–2300, closed Sun

Funky new bar tucked into a quiet street that nestles just off busy George Street. Attached restaurant offers a good choice of starters and mains, including a selection of chef's specials.

NB's ⑲

Balmoral Hotel, 1 Princes St

Bus 1, 10, 12, 15

Open: Mon–Thu 1000–1200, Fri 1000–0100, Sat 0900–0100, Sun 1100–2400

Hotel bar that welcomes passing tourists with open arms. Relaxed ambience, but at the same time a very polished feel that translates to snack-type food.

The desserts are more impressive than the savoury choices in a bar that makes a worthwhile stop if the prospect of an expensive meal at the No. 1 restaurant downstairs scares your bank manager.

Standing Order ⑳

62–66 George St

Bus 13

Open: Mon–Sat 1100–0100, Sun 1230–0100

Another bank head-quarters given the conversion treatment. The décor is still as grand and seems to draw in more businessmen than it ever did when it was used for banking. A full bar menu is on offer to accompany a good range of drinks in a venue where you have the chance to meet plenty of Edinburgh's business community letting its hair down after work.

THE NEW TOWN
Shops, markets and picnic sites

Shops

Glass & Thompson ㉑

2 Dundas St

🚍 Bus 23

Open: Mon–Sat 0830–1730, Sun 1100–1630

This is the fine food shop where the upper classes of Edinburgh's New Town flock to buy the goodies for their dinner parties. Join the throng and discover a wide range of delights with a loose Mediterranean theme.

Hanover Health Foods ㉒

40 Hanover St

🚍 Bus 23

Open: Mon–Sat 0930–1730, closed Sun

Tiny shop situated down below busy Hanover Street in a basement. As well as health remedies and herbal teas, it also stocks muesli, rice cakes, cereals, organic wheat bran, Macsweens vegetarian haggis, tofu, wholemeal flour and 'Pure Scottish Heather Honey'.

Jenners ㉓

48 Princes St

🚍 Bus 1, 10, 12, 15

Open: Mon–Wed 0900–1730, Thu 0900–1930, Fri–Sat 0900–1800, Sun 1200–1700

Edinburgh's famous grand department store has long been a local favourite. The in-store food shop is a smaller version of that found in London's Harrods, but of similar quality with the best of Scottish produce, including Macsweens haggis and many well-sourced own label foods. Jenners is quality shopping with a real sense of occasion.

Margiotta ㉔

71 Northumberland St

🚍 Bus 23

Open: Mon–Sat 0730–2200, Sun 0800–2200

Margiotta is a cross between a grocer and a delicatessen and has a number of branches across the city, though arguably this one is the best. Here you will find a wide variety of typically Scottish food-stuffs, including Baxters soup, Macsweens haggis and a selection of **Henderson's** (*see page 56*) pre-prepared vegetarian food.

▲ Jenners

Marks and Spencer 25

54 Princes St

🚌 Bus 1, 10, 12, 15

Open: Mon–Wed 0930–
1900, Thu 0900–2000, Fri
0900–1900, Sat 0830–
1800, Sun 1200–1700

The basement of this
branch of the world-
renowned department
store is devoted to food
and drink. Choose from
a top-notch range of
sandwiches, drinks and
fresh fruit, all packaged
and ready to take away
for a picnic across the
road in Princes Street
Gardens.

Paneficio Italiano Patisserie 26

7 Baker's Pl

🚌 Bus 23

Open: Mon–Sat 0700–1730,
closed Sun

A small Italian bakery
in trendy Stockbridge,
which stocks a good
range of freshly cooked
breads as well as ready-
made Italian staples
such as *bruschetta* and
pizza slices to take back
to your room. As well
as a good selection of
savouries there are also
some tempting sugary
treats.

Princes Mall 27

By Waverley Station

🚌 most buses

Open: Mon–Wed, Fri 0900–
1700, Thu 0900–2000, Sat
0900–1730, Sun 1000–
1600

A sprawling network of
shops set around a not
unpleasant pond in the

▲ Princes Street Gardens

bowels of Princes Street.
There are plenty of
options on the multitude
of floors.

Rowland's 28

42 Howe St

🚌 Bus 29, 29A

Open: Mon–Fri 0800–1500,
Sat 0900–1500, closed Sun

Small deli that sells
some interesting items.
It produces many of its
own jars of vinegar,
extra virgin olive oil
and pickles, including
an 'explosively hot
chilli pickle'. Organic
smoked salmon and the
exotic-sounding wild
boar terrine is also
sold here.

Sainsbury's Central 29

9–10 St Andrew's Sq

🚌 Bus 11

Open: Mon–Sat 0700–2100,
Sun 1000–1900

This new supermarket
opened in early 2000,
next to Jenners and
near Marks and Spencer,
trying to corner the
same picnic crowd
during the warmer
months. A great range
of sandwiches and light
meals is on offer, as

well as enough basic
items to keep most
people happy. Takeaway
coffee is also available,
and generally this shop
is the cheapest of the
three picnic options.

Picnic sites

Princes Street Gardens 30

🚌 Bus 1, 10, 12, 15

Open: until dusk

The famous gardens are
split into two halves by
the Mound. The western
half has a fountain,
bandstand and carousel,
while the smaller
eastern section has a
putting green. Both
offer wooden benches
and plenty of space on
the grass and, of course,
share those unforget-
table views of the castle
and the Old Town. Grab
a picnic and join the
crowds heading down to
the gardens in summer
or just buy an ice cream
once you get there.
Concerts and special
events are often held in
the gardens during
summer and Festival
time.

Child-friendly restaurants

Food for the family

There is nothing worse when you are on holiday than being turned away from a restaurant with your family in tow. There is no need for this ever to happen in Edinburgh as there is a wide choice of restaurants at all levels catering for families and children. Many restaurants also have special children's menus and the city has the usual number of international fast-food outlets, guaranteed to please the young ones.

One factor to bear in mind is that many of the city's bars and pubs do not allow children under the age of 18 on the premises, and some even bar those under the age of 21, though these rules are often flouted, depending on the time of day and how busy the establishment is.

One of the best places in town to take the children to is **Guiliano's** (*1 Commercial St; ✆ 0131 554 5272;* ❷❷) on the Shore. At weekends this popular Italian restaurant is taken over by families coming out for a meal or to celebrate birthdays. The walls echo constantly to the strains of piped renditions of *Happy Birthday* and other child-friendly songs as the staff make a real effort to entertain the youngsters. Despite all the horseplay, the food is fantastic, with pizza and pasta dishes overflowing with fresh ingredients and strong flavours that will put a smile on the faces of older diners.

If the children like ice cream, then they will be in heaven from the moment they step into **Lucas** (*16 Morningside Rd; ✆ 0131 446 0233;* ❶). Until recently, if you wanted to taste what many people rate as Scotland's best ice cream, you had to journey out to Musselborough. They have now opened an Edinburgh branch, with an ice-cream counter downstairs and an informal café upstairs. The menu is light and fun, but all a bit of a prelude to the desserts. The ice cream comes in a huge variety of forms, including the unbelievably indulgent Knickerbockerglory, a riot of ice cream, cream, jelly and

fruit. Little touches such as giving the children a Disney cup to take away with them make all the difference. On warm days, consider buying an ice cream and strolling down through Bruntsfield Links to the Meadows.

If you are down in Leith or visiting the royal yacht *Britannia*, then **Harry Ramsden's** (*Newhaven Rd; ✆ 0131 551 5566;* ❸❸) is close at hand to keep the children happy. This branch of the national chain dishes up all the mainstays, including the perennially popular fish and chips. Children are well looked after, though the service can be a bit poor when the restaurant is busy. On sunny summer days they also have tables outside.

Another good family option down in Leith is **Umbertos** (*Bonnington Rd; ✆ 0131 554 1314;* ❸❸). Downstairs, there is a good Italian restaurant to keep parents happy, but the whole upper floor is devoted to keeping more precocious visitors entertained. Children seem genuinely to lose themselves here as they grapple with the toy train and the smorgasbord of fun things to do.

The **Bridge Inn** (*Canal Centre, Ratho; ✆ 0131 333 1320;* ❸ *Glasgow express buses from St Andrew's Sq (buses at frequent intervals) or taxi*) is a fair way out of town, but it offers a good family eating choice and the children can play by the canal

afterwards, or you can even go on a canal cruise. As well as good pub grub for the grown-ups, there is a separate children's menu and a dedicated play area outside.

> The walls echo constantly to the strains of piped renditions of *Happy Birthday* and other child-friendly songs as the staff make a real effort to entertain the young.

Another good out-of-town option is down at the relaxed suburb of Cramond, just on the outskirts of the city. This pretty village rests on the edge of the Firth of Forth and the River Almond. Here you will find the **Cramond Brig Hotel** (*Queensferry Rd, Barton, Edinburgh EH4 8AP; ✆ 0131 339 4350;* ❸ *bus 40, 41, 41A;* ❸), an oasis if your children are driving you mad. They make a lot of effort to keep younger diners happy with a children's playground both inside and outdoors.

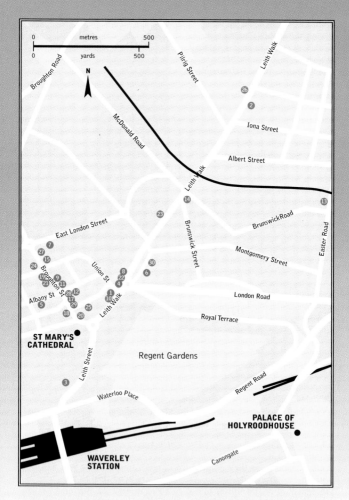

Leith Walk and Broughton Street

Leith Walk can at best be described as 'gritty' as all attempts to clean up the street seem to have failed. Don't make the mistake of many locals, though, who steer clear, as the southern end of Leith Walk has some great restaurants and delis, and Broughton Street is easily the city's liveliest eating and drinking enclave.

LEITH WALK AND BROUGHTON STREET
Restaurants

bleu ❶

4/8 Union St

✆ 0131 557 8451

🚍 Bus 7, 14, 16, 17, 22

Open: daily, 1200–1500, 1800–2300

Reservations recommended

💳 💳

Scottish/French

€

Rising from the ashes of the Pierre Victoire restaurant on the same site, this trendy French eatery claims to want to do away with the traditional three-course meal. Instead, you are offered *bouchées*, which are a French version of Spanish *tapas racions*. If you are hungry, you can have a selection of *bouchées* or even double or banquet *bouchées*. It may all sound a bit gimmicky, but the food is excellent.

Caprice ❷

325–331 Leith Wlk

✆ 0131 554 1279

🚍 Bus 7, 14, 16, 17, 22

Open: daily, 1200–1400, 1730–2300, Sun 1800–2300

💳 💳

All credit cards accepted

Italian

€

Caprice used to be one of the in-places in this part of town, but has long since been overtaken by the funky new eateries in Broughton Street. What Caprice

does offer today is some of the best pizzas in town, cooked in wood-burning ovens, with tasty thin bases. Few tourists and a minimum of fuss leaves you free to enjoy the pizzas.

Craigs

King James Thistle Hotel, St James Centre, 1 Leith St

✆ 0131 556 0111

🚍 Bus 7, 14, 16, 17, 22

Open: daily, 1230–1400, 1830–2200

Reservations recommended

All credit cards accepted

Scottish

€

St James Centre may be regarded by many locals as Edinburgh's ugliest building, but this hotel restaurant is handy if you are shopping in the centre itself. It has a 'shopper's lunch' and other good-value menus throughout the day, making this a good place to stop if you are in the area.

Ferri's Restaurant ❹

1 Antigua St

✆ 0131 556 5592

🚍 Bus 7, 14, 16, 17, 22

Open: Mon–Thu 1200–1400, 1700–2400, Fri–Sat 1200–0230, Sun 1700–2400

Reservations recommended

Italian

€

If you are catching a show or concert at the Playhouse Theatre, this is an excellent trattoria-style restaurant to pop in to before or after-wards, thanks to its late opening at weekends. The simple décor is a refreshing change from tacky Italian kitsch. After a lazy evening meal here you will feel part of the family that runs this popular eatery.

Haldane's ❺

39A Albany St

✆ 0131 556 8407

🚌 Bus 7, 14, 16, 17, 22

Open: Mon–Thu 1200–1400, 1800–2130, Fri 1200–1400, 1800–2230, Sat 1800–2230, Sun 1800–2130

Reservations recommended

All credit cards accepted

Scottish

€€

An oasis of Georgian calm just off the multi-ethnic, multi-sexual world of Broughton Sreet. Haldane's has that country house pour-a-drink-by-the-fire ambience. Chef George Kelso ensures that the food is very much on the traditional side of things, making the restaurant perfect for that ultimate Scottish experience.

Jolly ❻

9 Elm Row

✆ 0131 556 1588

🚌 Bus 7, 14, 16, 17, 22

Open: Mon–Sat 1200–1430, 1700–2300, Sun 1700–2230

Reservations recommended

All credit cards accepted

Italian

€

Another relaxed pizzeria that is blessed with a wood-burning oven. This is the sort of friendly local restaurant that will make Italian visitors feel at home as their pizzas are served up with a smile in simple surroundings.

Lost Sock Diner ❼

11 East London St

✆ 0131 557 6097

🚌 Bus 7, 14, 16, 17, 22

Open: Mon 0900–1600, Tue–Sat 0900–2200, Sun 1000–1700

Reservations recommended

International

€

A unique restaurant-cum-bistro where you can eat while you do your washing at the adjacent laundrette. Look for the decorative socks hanging in the window and you cannot miss the restaurant. This quirky place has a surprisingly diverse menu, with everything from burgers through to sun-dried vegetable sandwiches. During the summer the place buzzes with arty types

relaxing at the outdoor tables and people heaving their washing in and out.

Mamma Roma ❽

4–5 Antigua St

✆ 0131 558 1628

🚌 Bus 7, 14, 16, 17, 22

Open: Sun–Thu 1200–1430, 1700–2300, Fri–Sat 1200–1430, 1700–2400

Reservations recommended

Italian

€

An authentic Italian restaurant just across the road from the Playhouse. This small, unfussy Italian does the basics, but does them well with pasta dishes the speciality.

Mediterrano ❾

73 Broughton St

✆ 0131 557 6900

🚌 Bus 7, 14, 16, 17, 22

Open: Mon–Wed 0730–1800, Thu–Sat 0730–2200, Sun 0930–1630

Reservations recommended

Mediterranean

€

A very relaxed restau-rant that is filled with people taking a break during the day. At night it fills up with couples and tourists looking for a similarly leisurely dinner.

Shezan Tandoori ❿

25 Union Pl

✆ 0131 557 5098

🚌 Bus 7, 14, 16, 17, 22

Open: Mon–Wed 1600–
2400, Thu–Sun 1200–1400,
1700–0030

Reservations recommended

Indian

ⓔ

A Tandoori-style restaurant that manages to pack in some fairly hot dishes as well as a good range of vegetarian options. Very laid-back atmosphere and a great place for a pre-Playhouse Theatre curry.

Smokestack

53–55A Broughton St

✆ 0131 556 6032

🚍 Bus 7, 14, 16, 17, 22

Open: Mon–Fri 1200–1430, 1800–2230, Sat 1200–2230, Sun 1200–1630, 1800–1930

Reservations recommended

American

ⓔ

Loosely styled Cajun and Creole cuisine that caters for a surprising number of palates, with everything from succulent steaks right through to spicy seafoods. The modern décor is impressive, with subtle lighting adding to the relaxing atmosphere. A very mixed clientele, but everyone is welcome.

Tapas Tree

1 Forth St

✆ 0131 556 7118

🚍 Bus 7, 14, 16, 17, 22

Open: daily, 1100–2300

Reservations recommended

Spanish

ⓔⓔ

Scotland meets Spain over the *tapas* table in this theme restaurant. Yes, you will find all the *tapas* usuals such as *chorizo* and *jamon serrano*, but these are catered towards the local palate. Somehow it still works and the traditional music and special theme nights make sure that the Tapas Tree is more than just a tacky theme eatery. A good place for a small group or if you want to get to know new friends better.

Tinelli

139 Easter Rd

✆ 0131 652 1932

🚍 Bus 7, 14, 16, 17, 22

Open: Mon–Sat 1200–1430, 1830–2300, closed Sun

Reservations recommended

Italian

ⓔ

Situated in an unlikely location near the home of one of the city's big two football teams, Hibernian, this Italian does not take the easy option and slip in a few pizzas and basic pastas on the menu. Instead, it opts to be a full trattoria, complete with hearty mains that would confound most people's image of Italian cuisine.

Vittoria

113 Brunswick St

✆ 0131 556 6171

🚍 Bus 7, 14, 16, 17, 22

Open: Mon–Sat 1000–2300, Sun 1200–2300

Reservations recommended

Italian

ⓔ

A Sicilian restaurant that doubles as a cosy local Italian through the chilly months, but then overflows with tourists in the summer. Whatever the time of year, you will get the same relaxed ambience, simple tasty food and friendly staff.

WOW

2 Broughton Pl

✆ 0131 558 8868

🚍 Bus 7, 14, 16, 17, 22

Open: Mon–Fri 1230–1500, 1800–2230, Sat 1200–1600, 1800–2300, Sun 1200–1600

Reservations recommended

All credit cards accepted

Scottish

ⓔ

One of the best eateries on increasingly popular Broughton Street. The food swings open Scotland's rich culinary larder and infuses it with neat twists in very mellow surrounds. Voluminous windows are great for people-watching from the candlelit tables.

LEITH WALK AND BROUGHTON STREET
Bars, cafés and pubs

Barony Bar 16

81–85 Broughton St

Bus 7, 14, 16, 17, 22

Open: Mon–Thu 1130–2400, Fri–Sat 1100–0030, Sun 1230–2300

A traditional bar nestling amongst the funky new bars on Broughton Street. Forget about fusion and avant-garde here as the menu sticks to home turf with a reliable range of such traditional foods as sandwiches and baked potatoes.

Baroque 17

39–41 Broughton St

Bus 7, 14, 16, 17, 22

Open: Mon–Sat 1000–0100, Sun 1200–0100

It looks like Antoni Gaudi has popped over from Spain himself to do the décor on this odd, but visually pleasing bar. Everywhere you look there are multi-coloured tiles and bizarre contorted twists of metal. The all-day menu leans back towards the Mediterranean, with wraps, seafood and spicy dishes ruling.

Basement 18

10A–12B Broughton St

Bus 7, 14, 16, 17, 22

Open: daily, 1200–0100

The Basement is one of the most popular bars

on trendy Broughton Street and it is easy to see why. The atmosphere is very laid-back, though the décor is a bit drab on a sunny day when outside looks far more tempting. The food is hearty, with a leaning toward Mexico and daily specials.

Blue Moon Café

1 Barony St

🚌 Bus 7, 14, 16, 17, 22

Open: Mon–Fri 1100–0030, Sat–Sun 0900–0030

Ostensibly a gay café, but the gregarious staff make a point of being straight-friendly. The thick warm colours make this a place where you can easily lose a whole afternoon without noticing. The menu takes its cues from Italy.

Catwalk Café

2 Picardy Pl

🚌 Bus 7, 14, 16, 17, 22

Open: daily, 1100–0100

Arguably the most stylish bar/café in Edinburgh, the Catwalk is used regularly for fashion shoots. Minimalism reigns with huge concrete slabs making a stairway to the darker space below. Most people come to drink or pose at the outdoor tables that seem to sneak out at the first sight of the sun at any time of the year. The culinary emphasis is on light Mediterranean-style dishes, with a good selection of sugary treats to savour with your *café latte* afterwards.

C32

32C Broughton St

🚌 Bus 7, 14, 16, 17, 22

Open: daily, 1030–2300

The new owners have brightened up the grey surrounds of the old DSK to make a bright, airy café. Blue chairs and paintings give it the feel of an IKEA store. Good value for light meals, especially breakfasts. Mainly gay, but they are also straight-friendly.

The Deep Sea

2 Antigua St

🚌 Bus 7, 14, 16, 17, 22

Open: Sun–Thu 1600–0130, Fri–Sat 1600–0200

Arguably the finest 'chippie' in the city, The Deep Sea has turned fish 'suppers' into an art form and attracts a dedicated following of regulars. If you want to see why Scotland's health record is so poor, come here and watch locals getting their hands on fried fish, chicken, sausages, black pudding and haggis. Pile on lashings of 'broon' sauce to complete the experience.

Embo

29 Haddington Pl

🚌 Bus 7, 14, 16, 17, 22

Open: Mon–Fri 0800–1800, Sat 1000–1700, closed Sun

Polished floors and polished Mediterranean staples are on offer at this classy deli. Excellent *panini* and gourmet sandwiches, with many vegetarian options. A wide range of coffees and freshly squeezed fruit juices.

Globe

42 Broughton St

🚌 Bus 7, 14, 16, 17, 22

Open: Mon–Fri 0700–1500, Sat 0800–1500, closed Sun

One of three branches of this great sandwich shop. Excellent value range of *focaccia*, filled rolls and baguettes. Interesting fillings such as *sopressa* salami with dolcelatte and Orkney cheddar with chutney.

The Outhouse

12A Broughton St Lane

🚌 Bus 7, 14, 16, 17, 22

Open: daily, 1200–0100

Just off the main Broughton Street throng, this is one of the area's trendiest bar/cafés. Minimalist décor and a with-it crowd make it a good place to have a lazy lunch and catch up on all the happenings in the city's vibrant music and club scene. The passable, though not inspiring, food is well presented and good value.

LEITH WALK AND BROUGHTON STREET
Shops, markets and picnic sites

Shops

Chinese Supermarket 26

310 Leith Wlk

🚌 Bus 7, 14, 16, 17, 22

Open: daily, 0900–1800

One of two Chinese supermarkets within metres of each other on opposite sides of Leith Walk. This one is smaller and friendlier, with all of the Chinese mainstays you would expect and cheap Tsing Tao beer as well.

Crombies 27

97 Broughton St

🚌 Bus 7, 14, 16, 17, 22

Open: Mon–Thu 0800–1800, Fri 0800–1900, Sat 0800–1700

For three generations Crombies has been synonymous with quality produce, with much of the extensive stock its own brand. The selection of sausages is claimed to be the widest of any shop in Scotland, with 35 varieties, including 'Caledonian', which is infused with Scottish ale. This is another good place where you can buy supplies for a picnic.

The Organic Food Shop 28

45 Broughton St

🚌 Bus 7, 14, 16, 17, 22

Open: Mon–Sat 1000–1830, closed Sun

This tiny shop is laden with fresh vegetables and fruits, as well as fresh garlic and spices. A good place to stock up on fruit for a picnic without paying supermarket prices and to find fresh vegetables if your accommodation has cooking facilities. Also sells organic baby foods, pasta sauces and fruit juices.

Real Foods 29

97 Broughton St

🚌 Bus 7, 14, 16, 17, 22

Open: Mon–Wed 0900–1900, Thu 0900–2230, Fri 0900–1900, Sat 0900–1830, Sun 1000–1800

Gluten-free, wheat-free and dairy-free is the slogan of this health-food shop. Its extensive range includes some fine breads, Macsweens vegetarian haggis and muesli and oats by the kilo.

Valvona & Crolla 30

19 Elm Row

🚌 Bus 7, 14, 16, 17, 22

Open: Mon–Wed 0800–1800, Thu–Fri 0800–1930, Sat 0800–1800, closed Sun

Legendary deli that for many locals is the best in the city. Worth a visit just for the smells, with an abundant supply of fresh goodies, including vegetables flown in daily from markets in Milan. Get the perfect picnic together here or just stock up on plump olives and a wonderful array of cheese and meats.

Souvenir foods

Head home with a haggis

Ask many people to list their images of Scotland and along with movies such as *Braveheart* and *Rob Roy*, and tartan and bagpipes, they will undoubtedly include **haggis**. This legendary food stuff is the most obvious foodie souvenir to take home from your trip and is always good for teasing your friends at home about the ingredients before you serve it up Scots-style with a dram of whisky and a word or two from Robert Burns, Scotland's national poet.

> Two of the best single-malt whiskies to take home with you are Glenfiddoch and Macallan, or, for true connoisseurs, Laiphroig and Talisker, where the real smokiness of the peat seeps through from every sip.

To many Scots haggis and Macsweens are synonymous. Macsweens is the most famous of the haggis producers and its range and quality never fails to impress, with vegetarian haggis to keep non-meat eaters happy. Sadly, its great deli outlet in Bruntsfield closed down recently, but you can still venture out of the city to visit **Macsweens' factory shop** (*Dryden Rd, Bilston Glen, Loanhead; ✆ 0131 440 2555; 🚍 buses 62, 64, 65 from the city centre; open: Mon–Fri 0830–1700*), an unusual excursion that few visitors know about. Here you can explore the secrets of the vegetarian haggis, which many Scots still think is a contradiction in terms. Out goes the meat and in its place are kidney beans, lentils, nuts, vegetables, as well as the traditional ingredients of oatmeal, onions and spices.

Scotland's other great product is **whisky**, which is one of the country's biggest exports. If you plan to buy a souvenir of the liquid the Scots call the 'water of life', then avoid the blended stuff that you can buy all over the world and invest in a single malt.

Two of the best are Glenfiddich and Macallan, or, for true connoisseurs, Laiphroig and Talisker, where the real smokiness of the peat seeps through from every sip. **Royal Mile Whiskies** (*379 High St, Royal Mile; ℘ 0131 225 3383*) has a massive range from which to choose, everything from inexpensive miniatures right through to rare single malts. The rarer malts make the best souvenirs as they are often impossible to track down outside of Scotland.

Shortbread is another great souvenir. This hard butter biscuit is sold in many forms throughout the city, from thin fingers to large circles smothered in sugar. The two most popular brands are Pattersons and Walkers, and their products seldom disappoint. Steer away from the tourist shops on the Royal Mile, however, as they charge through the roof for even the smallest box of shortbread.

Another sweet souvenir is **Edinburgh Rock**. This sugary treat is distinct from the rock sold elsewhere in the country by its chalky texture. You can buy it in box form in **Jenners** (*48 Princes St; open: Mon–Wed 0900–1730, Thu 0900–1930, Fri–Sat 0900–1800, Sun 1200–1700*) as well as from the **Tourist Information Office** (*3 Princes St*) and many of the tourist shops on the Royal Mile, though they usually hike up the price.

If you are not travelling too far, then Scottish **smoked salmon** is worth considering as a real culinary souvenir. Rated as some of the finest salmon in the world, it is best served up simply with a squeeze of lemon or on a bagel

with cream cheese. You will find it on sale at most supermarkets as well as in the city's delis and Jenners. You can also buy it at the airport to ensure that it remains as fresh as possible.

If you are in a hurry, the food shop inside Edinburgh's grand old department store, **Jenners** (*see page 64*), stocks a good range of foods, most neatly packaged, which make excellent gifts, along with an interesting range of haggis.

If your visit to Edinburgh has sparked an interest in Scottish cooking, then why not buy a Scottish cookbook? There is a wide range available, stretching from traditional cooking manuals through to funky modern Scottish ideas. The two branches of **Waterstone's** bookshops on Princes Street are good places to browse.

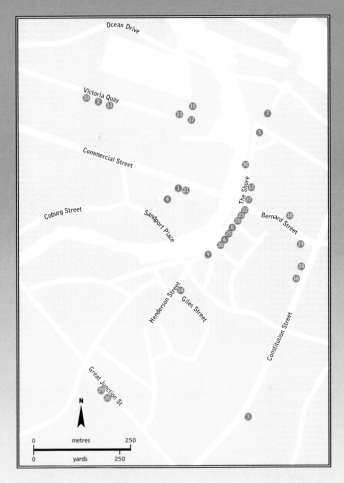

Leith

The riverside suburb of Leith managed to resurrect itself in the late 1990s as an example of urban regeneration. Despite the influx of top-class restaurants and warehouse conversions, rumours of places closing down continually ripple through Leith. The arrival of the Royal Yacht Britannia in 1998 and the new multi-million pound Ocean Terminal may finally see Leith emerge as the place to eat.

LEITH
Restaurants

La Camargue ❶

23 Commercial St

✆ 0131 554 9999

🚌 Bus 10A, 22

Open: daily, 1900–2200

Reservations recommended

All credit cards accepted

French

❶❷

Classic French cuisine served up in comfort-able surroundings. The chefs follow the Leith theme and specialise in seafood, including an excellent Dover *sole meunière*. A great range of French wines helps make this a special place for dinner.

Daniel's Bistro ❷

88 Commercial St

✆ 0131 553 5933

🚌 Bus 10A, 22

Open: Sun–Thu 1200–2130, Fri–Sat 1200–2130

Reservations essential

All credit cards accepted

French

❶❷

Run by the man who was behind the legendary L'Auberge, this more informal

RESTAURANT
MARTIN WISHART

restaurant is now attracting its own dedicated following. The French-bistro style cooking is impressive, drawing upon a wide selection of ingredients, including, perhaps unsurprisingly, seafood, as is the norm for this part of town. Expect to experience elements of Scottish and French cooking merging on your plate.

Denzlers ❸

121 Constitution St	
✆ 0131 554 3268	
🚍 Bus 10A, 22	
Open: Mon–Fri 1200–1400, 1830–2200, Sat 1830–2200, closed Sun	
Reservations recommended	
All credit cards accepted	
Swiss	
❻	

The only Swiss restaurant in the city, whose walls are somewhat incongruously attired with Scottish paintings. It makes a pleasant change in Edinburgh to steer clear of funky new eateries and gorge on mains smothered with Swiss cheese and traditional Swiss desserts like strudel. If you are lucky, you may just be in town for one of its Swiss wine-tasting evenings.

Domenicos ❹

30 Sandport St	
✆ 0131 467 7266	
🚍 Bus 10A, 22	
Open: Mon–Thu 1200–1400, 1830–2200, Fri 1200–1400, 1830–2230, Sat 1200–2230, Sun 1200–2200	
Reservations recommended	
All credit cards accepted	
Italian	
❻	

Domenicos is a world away from the glossy eateries in trendy Commercial Quay. This family-run Italian does the simple things well and attracts a dedicated following of locals as a result. You cannot go wrong with the well-prepared pasta dishes.

Fishers ❺

1 The Shore	
✆ 0131 554 5666	
🚍 Bus 10A, 22	
Open: daily, 1215–1600, 1800–2230	
Reservations essential	
All credit cards accepted	
Seafood	
❻ ❻	

Great opening hours and top-class seafood make this a firm local favourite. So much so that Tony Blair popped in during a visit to Edinburgh. There are two rooms, one with windows looking out over the Leith, and the other a darker affair where you can eat at the bar.

Kavios ❻

63 The Shore	
✆ 0131 467 7746	
🚍 Bus 10A, 22	
Open: daily, 1100–2300	
Reservations recommended	
Italian	
❻	

Although this Italian restaurant does not look very special from the outside, and it is not much more appealing décor-wise on the inside, the sturdy cuisine does not disappoint on the plate. This is an Italian where you can leave the pizzas and pastas behind, with a variety of seafood, including monkfish and red snapper, given the Italian treatment.

Malmaison Brasserie

1 Tower Pl

✆ 0131 468 5001

🚍 Bus 10A, 22

Open: Mon–Fri 0700–1000, 1200–1430, 1800–2230, Sat 0800–1030, 1200–1430, 1800–2230, Sun 0800–1030, 1200–1430, 1800–2200

Reservations recommended

🆅🆂🅰 American Express

French

💷💷

Enjoy the lively turn-of-the-century brasserie-style ambience in this stunningly converted modern hotel. The menu changes every six weeks, but always relies on innovative and fresh French cooking. There is a decent wine and champagne list and first-class *crème brûlée*. The Malmaison is a great venue to enjoy a classy, good-value meal, before exploring Leith's pubs. A meal and a night spent here will take you right to the heart of

Leith's recent unlikely renaissance. Also available is a private salon for groups of 6 to 16, often with no extra room charge.

Martin Wishart ⑧

54 The Shore

✆ 0131 553 3557

🚍 Bus 10A, 22

Open: Sun–Fri 1200–1430, 1900–2230, Sat 1900–2230

Reservations essential

All credit cards accepted except ⊙

Scottish

💷💷

One of Edinburgh's best chefs with all the right contacts, Martin Wishart still has a major hand in this stylish outlet. The neat, small restaurant is booked solid at weekends with locals who come time and time again to enjoy the first-rate culinary experience on offer.

The Raj ⑨

91 Henderson Street

✆ 0131 553 3980

🚍 Bus 10A, 22

Open: Sun–Thu 1200–1430, 1730–2330, Fri–Sat 1200–1430, 1730–2400

Reservations recommended

All credit cards accepted

Indian

💷

The Shore may have been largely taken over by classy, expensive restaurants, but the Raj is a good budget option. Unsurprisingly, a colonial feel given the

name, but the décor somehow manages not to be too overpowering. A good range of regional Indian cuisines is on offer, and if you like the delicious chutneys you can always take them home with you as they are sold in jars.

Rajdhani ⑩

Unit 9, Commercial Quay

✆ 0131 553 1518

🚍 Bus 10A, 22

Open: daily 1200–1430, 1730–2300

Reservations recommended

🆅🆂🅰 American Express

Indian

💷

A decent Indian restaurant formerly known as the Joypur until its recent name change. Its speciality is *Rajdhani Bahaar*, chicken cooked in a clay oven in a special chef's sauce. Excellent value set-lunch menus and big portions are a further attraction.

The Rock ⑪

78 Commercial St

✆ 0131 555 2225

🚍 Bus 10A, 22

Open: Tue–Sat 1200–1400, 1830–2200, closed Sun–Mon

Reservations recommended

All credit cards accepted

Scottish

💷💷

Smartly designed modern restaurant serving smartly

▲ The Ship on the Shore

designed modern Scottish food. Attention focuses on the charcoal grill, which is always ready to cook what you want exactly the way you want it. An added bonus is being able to see all the machinations of the kitchens while you wait for your meal.

The Ship on the Shore 🕑

24–26 The Shore

✆ 0131 555 0409

🚍 Bus 10A, 22

Open: Sun–Thu 1200–2400, Fri 1200–0100, Sat 1100–0100

Reservations recommended

All credit cards accepted

Seafood

❷❻

Stranded alone now that the Ship, which lies just outside, is closed. Fortunately, the seafood here is as good as any along the seafront though it is noticeably

more casual in dress sense than the others. Cosy décor.

Skippers 🕓

1A Dock Pl

✆ 0131 554 1018

🚍 Bus 10A, 22

Open: Mon–Thu 1230–1400, 1900–2200, Fri–Sat 1230–1400, 1900–2230, Sun 1230–1430

Reservations essential

All credit cards accepted

Seafood

❷❻

In the minds of many locals this is the best seafood restaurant in Edinburgh and it is indeed hard to fault. It has a very atmospheric interior, with nautical bric-à-brac dotted all over the walls. Look out for the 'Britannia' dessert, a tribute to the former royal yacht that recently moved north to moor as a floating museum in Leith.

Vinter's Rooms 🕙

The Vaults, 87 Giles St

✆ 0131 554 6767

🚍 Bus 10A, 22

Open: Mon–Sat 1200–1400, 1900–2200, closed Sun

Reservations recommended

VISA 💳 American Express

French

❷❻

In this atmospheric and romantic restaurant, one room is lit solely by candlelight, which makes it an ideal spot for that perfect romantic meal. The other room is slightly less intimate. Using the best of local seafood the chef skilfully avoids the tendency to overcook and over-elaborate by sticking to the dictates of French provincial cooking.

Waterfront 🕘

1C Dock Pl

✆ 0131 554 7427

🚍 Bus 10A, 22

Open: Mon–Thu 1200–2300, Fri–Sat 1200–2400, Sun 1230–2230

Reservations recommended

All credit cards accepted

Seafood

❷❻

If the sun is shining you will not regret heading here and savouring a meal in the vine-covered conservatory. Even if it is overcast, the seafood is still first rate and there is enough choice on the menu to cater for both vegetarians and carnivores.

LEITH
Bars, cafés and pubs

Bar Java 16

48–50 Constitution St

Bus 10A, 22

Open: Mon–Wed 0700–2400, Thu–Fri 0700–0100, Sat–Sun 0800–2400

One of Leith's bright, funky new bars that also does a decent line in food. All-day breakfasts are popular, as are more substantial mains like salmon fillet and heaped plates of nachos. A buzzing place at weekends with live bands and a great place for Sunday brunch as Leith's 'in' crowd surfaces late to leaf through the Sunday newspapers.

Bar Sirius 17

7–10 Dock Pl

Bus 10A, 22

Open: Mon–Wed 1200–2400, Thu–Sun 1200–0100

This trendy bar is overflowing with young professionals and creative types. It buzzes at the weekends as the pre-clubbing set meet up before moving on. It also remains eternally popular for lazy lunches with Mexican wraps the big seller and breakfasts. Perfect for a drink pre- or post- a meal on Commercial Quay. Very busy most nights.

Bource 18

28 Bernard St

Bus 10A, 22

Open: Mon–Wed 0900–2300, Thu–Sun 0900–2400

Bright new space just back from the big-name restaurants on the Shore. The décor is minimalist, but still very comfortable. The menu is a strange mix of hearty pub grub and more ambitious efforts such as salmon steaks. A good place for lunch or even just to relax with one of the good selection of coffees.

Burns Alehouse 19

7 Bernard St

Bus 10A, 22

Open: daily, 1100–2300

This eatery is themed around Scotland's famed national poet, Robert Burns, author of *Auld Lang Syne* and countless better poems and ditties. The works of Burns bedeck the walls and tables in a pub that also does excellent bistro-style food. Try the cock-a-leekie soup and the rosti-style mains, and wash it all down with one of the extensive range of single malts on offer. A bit off the main tourist track, but well worth the effort.

Café Truva 20

77 The Shore

Bus 10A, 22

Open: Mon–Fri 0900–1700, Sat 1000–1730, Sun 1030–1730

Turkish-run café tucked on the waterfront offering good-value meals. The small menu includes homemade lamb moussaka and quiche, as well as a limited range of coffees and sweets.

Cameo Bar 21

23 Commercial St

Bus 10A, 22

Open: daily, 1200–0100

Owned by the same people as the adjacent **La Camargue** restaurant (*see page 79*), this trendy bar has its own basic menu that revolves around burgers, chips and nachos. It also has a big screen for major sporting events.

Kings Wark 22

36 The Shore

Bus 10A, 22

Open: Mon–Thu 1200–2300, Fri–Sat 1200–2400, Sun 1100–2300

Very atmospheric old pub where you will feel as though the 20th, never mind the 21st, century has never started. Good restaurant in one half, but even

you can sample a wide range of ales, which includes a good selection of English 'bitters', as well as a selection of decent bar food.

Port o' Leith 24

58 Constitution St

Bus 10A, 22

Open: Mon–Sat 1200–2400, Sun 1200–1100

One of Leith's real experiences as you encounter the unique hospitality of the off-beat owner, Mary Moriarty. This is unreconstructed Leith, a world away from funky furniture and smooth service. Pull up a stool, grab a beer, choose a bar snack and then sit back and take in the atmospheric surroundings and enjoy the local patois.

Waterside 25

58 The Shore

Bus 10A, 22

Open: Mon–Thu 1200–1400, Fri–Sat 1200–0100, Sun 1230–2400

Opened in March 2000, this bright bar used to be the moody old Leith Oyster Bar. The new incarnation serves up a decent range of food at inexpensive prices for the Shore. Fish and chips and burgers abound and the excellent Czech beers Budvar and Staropramen are available on draught.

better value bar food to a very high standard in the pub area. Working your way through fish and chips and a pint of heavy as the River Leith lazes by only metres away is a true Leith experience.

Malt and Hops 23

45 The Shore

Bus 10A, 22

Open: Mon–Wed 1200–2300, Thu 1200–2400, Fri–Sat 1200–0100, Sun 1230–1100

An open fire welcomes in those wandering along the River Leith. This is a real pub whose walls are laden with beer mats. Malt and Hops claims to be the oldest bar in the city, but other landlords may dispute this claim. Here

LEITH
Shops, markets and picnic sites

Shops

JAS Anderson 26

51 Great Junction St

Bus 10A, 22

Open: Mon–Sat 0700–1700, closed Sun

A real traditional butcher, offering all the Scottish staples. They claim, rather immodestly, to make the best haggis in the country, and also do a good line in steaks, mince, black pudding and corned beef.

The Clock 27

35 The Shore

Bus 10A, 22

Open: Mon–Fri 0800–1500, Sat 0900–1500, closed Sun

Simple shop amongst the expensive restaurants of The Shore in Leith. Stock up on your sandwich ingredients as well as *focaccia*, Italian rolls and croissants. A couple of seats are available if you want to eat in. Takeaway coffee is available by the flask, which is handy for picnics.

Fleur's Deli 28

52 The Shore

Bus 10A, 22

Open: Mon–Sat 0800–1500, Sun 0900–1500

Very basic food shop that has been running for over a decade. The menu features around 100 sandwiches as well as croissants and toasties. Also has fresh fruit and general food stuffs for sale.

Food Junction 29

59 Great Junction St

Bus 10A, 22

Open: Mon–Sat 0900–1800, closed Sun

A surprisingly diverse range of food and drink is available here, given the shabby shops and bars that fill up the rest of this street in unreconstructed Leith. Alongside the usual fruit and vegetables you will find more exotic items such as chillies and pak choi, as well as kale, a traditional Scottish green.

Picnic sites

The Shore 30

Bus 10A, 22

Open: all day

Grab a picnic from one of the nearby shops and then head to a bench by the River Leith. From here you can appreciate the scale of the regeneration the area has undergone. You can appreciate the contrasts of troubled Leith, with the more gritty housing areas crowding right on the edge of the new glamorous Leith.

Out-of-town restaurants

The quiet life

Edinburgh is blessed with so many great restaurants in such a compact area that it is very tempting not to take the trouble to travel out of the city centre on your Epicurean adventures. If you have the time, though, there are some excellent restaurants just a short journey away from the city. Getting to these selections is a lot easier if you have your own car, but they are all accessible using a combination of public transport and taxis

From the pre-dinner drink before a roaring fire to a post-dinner coffee upstairs in the Tapestry Room, a meal at Prestonfield House Hotel is sheer indulgence.

Prestonfield House Hotel (*Priestfield Rd; ✆ 0131 668 3346; open: daily, 1200–1400, 1700–2100;* ◉ *taxi from city centre;* ❶❷❸) offers a real flavour of the Scottish Highlands just a 10-minute taxi ride from the centre of town. This elegant country house combines sweeping views of Arthur's Seat and more gentle views of the countryside, with Highland cows and peacocks roaming the grounds. From the pre-dinner drink before a roaring fire to a post-dinner coffee upstairs in the Tapestry Room, a meal here is sheer indulgence. The Old Dining Room is very over the top, with plush red chairs and neo-classical pillars, but it still manages to stay on the right side of Scottish kitsch. The food is a robust menu of Scottish mainstays, well cooked and presented with polished service.

Another charming country house can be found further out of the city, at **Houston Hotel** (*Uphall, West Lothian; ✆ 01506 853831; open: Sun–Fri 1200–1400, 1900–2130, Sat 1900–2130;* ◉ *bus 16, 17, 18 from St Andrew's Sq or a taxi;* ❶❷❸). Set in 20 acres (8 hectares) of grounds, this elegant stone-washed building swirls in tall stories about Mary, Queen of Scots and is laden with atmosphere. Pre-dinner drinks are served in cosy surroundings before you venture upstairs into the formal dining room that looks as though it has not changed in centuries. The food infuses traditional Scottish cuisine with a few neat twists and the wine list is excellent. Go the whole hog and stay the night for a real treat.

La Potinière (*Main St, Gullane; ✆ 01620 843214; ☻ call for current details; ❷❷*) is around 19 miles (30km) west of the city centre and is well worth the effort of getting there. The style of food is loosely classified as French/Scottish crossover, but it is constantly evolving depending on what is in season. There are some decent golf courses nearby so you may want to make a day of it if you are a golf fanatic.

Another highly rated eatery is situated in the middle of nowhere, but easily accessible from the historic town of Linlithgow. **Champany's Hotel** (*near Linlithgow; ✆ 01506 834532; open: daily 1230–1400, 1930–2200; ☻ train to Linlithgow from Waverley Station; for information and ticket prices, call 08705 484950, then taxi to Champany's; ❷❷*) has been pulling in the locals for years with its eclectic culinary treats. Yes, you can choose to chomp on the huge steaks that it is rightly famed for, but you can also opt for other treats such as the fresh lobster.

If you are looking for an informal meal outside the city that will not stretch your holiday budget as much, then head to East Linton and the welcoming arms of the **Drover's Inn** (*5 Bridge St, East Linton; ✆ 01620 860298; open: Mon–Thu 1130–2400, Fri–Sat 1130–0100, Sun 1230–2400; ☻ bus 106 from St Andrew's Sq to East Linton, hourly service; call to enquire about their courtesy bus; ❷❷*).

If you want to sample a slice of provincial Scottish life, this is it, with friendly service and equally friendly locals. On summer days venture south of Edinburgh and sip on a beer in the beer garden as you tuck into the hearty fare.

The **Hawes Inn** (*see page 47*) is also a great out-of-town pub, with above-average food and a beer garden where you can sit outside by the Firth of Forth watching the ships head off to sea, while the trains trundle over the world-famous Forth Rail Bridge above. This pub is laden with atmosphere, as is the surrounding town, making it a great venue for an afternoon out of the city or a night away.

▲ Houston Hotel

Food etiquette and culture

A new approach to food and eating

The last decade or so has seen a seismic shift in the way many Scottish people think about food and drink. Nowhere has this been more pronounced than in Edinburgh. Gone are the days when the choice was either between 'meat and two veg' at home or a quick visit to the local 'chippie' for some greasy fast food. Interest in food in itself, rather than just looking on meal times as a necessity, has risen sharply in recent years with cooking programmes on television and cooking courses

becoming ever more popular. Edinburgh today is a cosmopolitan city overflowing with a myriad of eating and drinking experiences, and a city whose culinary reputation is rising year on year.

There are usually three main meals a day in Edinburgh, with the main meal being eaten in the evening. Looking at Scotland's horrific statistics on coronary heart disease, you might imagine that most Scots start the day with a cooked breakfast, but many locals in Edinburgh today opt instead for cereal, a croissant or a pastry, with a number of eateries recently opening up in the city to cater for this new demand. Lunch is usually taken from 1200 through to 1400, with Edinburgh's restaurants often closing down after this. Dinner is then usually fairly early, between 1700 and 1900 if eaten at home or 1900 and 2100 in the city's restaurants. 'High Tea' seems to have disappeared.

WHAT TO WEAR

When it comes to etiquette most restaurants veer towards informality. There are few major faux pas that you can make and not many restaurants insist on a jacket and tie. Smart casual attire is generally the norm.

TIPPING AND SERVICE

Tipping at around 10 per cent is the standard, as most restaurants don't factor a service charge into the bill. If service has been particularly bad, leaving no tip at all is acceptable.

Much has been made in the Scottish media of late about poor standards of service in restaurants and other tourist industries, but the standard in Edinburgh is usually fairly high, though it can be on the slow side. In ethnic restaurants it is totally acceptable to ask for a knife and fork if you do not feel comfortable with chopsticks. One poor aspect of service that still seems to affect many restaurants, even at the top level, is that customers' complaints are often taken personally or result in surly service. By law, all restaurants must display a current menu on the exterior of the restaurant.

CODE OF CONDUCT

While Edinburgh's restaurants are relatively informal, the pubs and bars by contrast have a strict in-built code that is easy to break. In many of the more traditional bars it is unheard of to order whisky with anything other than a dash of water. The real purists believe that ice dulls the full flavour and mixing a decent malt with a soft drink is nothing short of sacrilege. In company, 'rounds' are the norm and it is considered rude not to offer everyone in the group – even people you have just met – a drink when you are going up to the bar.

OPENING HOURS

In terms of opening times, the

main days that Scots go out for a meal are Thursdays, Fridays and Saturdays, with restaurant hours revolving around this. As Edinburgh is a very popular tourist destination, there is always something open to satisfy most tastes. The traditional holy day of Sunday no longer closes all restaurants, with most operating on reduced opening hours. Most bars and pubs also close earlier on Sunday nights. Visitors from large cities in Europe and America will quickly observe that Edinburgh is not yet a 24-hour city, though there are still a few late-night eating options. Opening hours for pubs and bars are generally far more liberal than those further south in England. You will seldom find it difficult to get a drink in Edinburgh as many bars and pubs stay open until at least midnight during the week and often until 0200 or 0300 at weekends.

Menu decoder

BISCUITS AND CAKES

bannocks – halfway between scones and pancakes

black bun – a peppery fruitcake encased within pastry. Particularly popular around Hogmanay (New Year)

Dundee cake – fruit cake, too rich for some, finished off with almonds. Popular during afternoon tea

oatcakes – popular oatmeal biscuits, often served with cheese at the end of a meal.

scones – light, fluffy buttermilk muffins, usually served with jam

shortbread – a very popular hard, buttery biscuit, served with everything from a dram of whisky or used as a dessert base

BREAD AND PANCAKES

butteries – buttery bread rolls native to the Aberdeenshire area

Scottish pancakes – small, thick pancakes served for breakfast or with afternoon tea

BREAKFAST AND SUPPER

Cooked breakfast/fry-up is still the way to start the day for many Scots. Includes some or all from a list of sausages, haggis, mushrooms, tattie scones, clootie dumpling, eggs, bacon, black pudding and tomatoes. Mercifully less popular than it was 10 years ago, but still an essential for most Scots when dealing with that dreaded Sunday morning feeling.

supper – adding chips to the fish, chicken, haggis, etc, on sale at a chippie. As in 'fish supper'

BROTHS, PORRIDGES AND SOUPS

cock-a-leekie soup – chicken and leek soup so beloved of grandmothers all over the nation, but making an unlikely comeback in classy restaurants

Cullen Skink – fish soup based around its main ingredient – smoked haddock. Again, a traditional dish making something of an unlikely comeback in Edinburgh's restaurants

porridge – traditional oatmeal breakfast, usually served hot with salt to add taste, though tourists are usually allowed a dash of sugar instead

powsowdie – sheep's head broth doesn't sound too appetising, but, like haggis, the taste is better than the concept

Scotch broth – traditional soup built around the staples of barley, lentils and stock

skirlie – oatmeal, dripping, leek and chicken stock mixed together to create a savoury porridge. Often served with poultry or pork

west coast broth – seafood soup originating from Scotland's wild west coast

CHEESE

Lanark Blue – famous as one of the nation's finest cheeses

unpasteurised cheese – a little bit of rebellion as Scots throw health concerns out of the window and dabble in this cheese produced the way farmers used to make it

CONDIMENTS

buckshot – a cracked black pepper and cream sauce that accompanies many dishes served up across the capital

grape chutney – this popular chutney features on menus in Edinburgh alongside a selection of cheese and oatcakes/bread at the end of the meal

DESSERTS AND PUDDINGS

Atholl brose – traditional dessert consisting of oatmeal, whisky and cream

clootie dumpling – a steamed pudding with currants and raisins that you will find served as a dessert and, bizarrely, in the midst of your morning fry-up

cranachan – thick fresh cream, oatmeal, whisky and fresh berries are combined in this wonderful traditional dessert that now graces Scotland's fine dining restaurants in its many variations. Drambuie has recently been edging out the whisky in a number of restaurants. Also sometimes served with cream cheese substituted for the thick cream

Drumlanrig pudding – rhubarb pudding similar to bread and butter pudding

DRINK

blended whisky – different whiskies are blended together to make the 'blend'. If it is done well it can be almost as good as malt, but poor blends give whisky its unwarranted firewater reputation. Common blends such as Bells and Grouse are good for mixing with soft drinks – usually Coca-Cola or Irn Bru

BYOB – bring your own bottle. Restaurants which allow you to bring along your own alcohol, though some may also levy a corkage charge for opening it and supplying glasses

Drambuie – quality Scots liqueur that is sold all over the world and is used in Edinburgh's restaurants as a flavouring in a variety of dishes, from steak sauces to desserts

Glayva – a Scottish liqueur that is increasing in popularity. A more herb taste compared to Drambuie, but also used in desserts. Makes an interesting ingredient in ice creams

heavy – very popular dark ale usually served uncarbonated and at cellar temperature. Comes in varying strengths represented on menus with a '/-'. The most common varieties are 70/- and 80/-

hot toddy – many a Scottish grandmother insists on this cold cure that has intoxicated many a cheerful young cold victim. The essentials are lemon, honey and, of course, whisky

Irn Bru – marketed as 'Scotland's other national drink', a very popular soft drink and renowned as a hangover cure

malt whisky – pure whisky, unblended, produced at a single distillery

pint and a hauf – a pint of ale or lager accompanied by a dram of whisky. The popular working man's way to drink, increasingly less popular as designer beers and lagers invade Edinburgh's pubs

Whisky-Mac – whisky served mixed with ginger wine, one of the few accompaniments to whisky that a barman won't grit his teeth and throw you a dirty look when you ask for it

FISH

Arbroath smokies – famed smoked haddock from Scotland's east coast

crayfish – also known as lobster, most commonly from Scotland's bountiful west coast waters

Finnan haddock – some of Scotland's best haddock, smoked whole with tail and skin left intact

kedgeree – haddock mixed with rice and eggs

Klabbi-Dhu – large horse mussels. Sourced from Scotland's north-western waters, these mussels are often served *moules marinières*-style

Krappin Heit – an unusual dish of cod's head stuffed with fish livers and oatmeal

Loch Fyne oysters – famous oysters from this Highland loch

partan – Scots name for crab

MEAT

Aberdeen Angus – the best of quality Scottish beef, famous around the world. An industry standard

Ayrshire bacon – renowned as the country's best bacon, originating in Robert Burns country

black pudding – a common type of sausage that relies heavily on the ingredient of dried blood, which gives it its colour

grouse – game bird available only in season. Very richly

flavoured meat that can be overpowering if not cooked well

haggis – the most famous Scottish dish – not, as many locals would have gullible tourists believe, a mythical beast that roams the Highlands! In reality, haggis is an unappetising sounding mix of sheep's stomach, heart, liver and other offal, lent its undoubted good taste with the addition of oatmeal and a variety of spices. Haggis is very much the nation's national dish

Lorne sausage – a square sausage that is usually fried. Sometimes appears in a cooked breakfast

pheasant – game bird available only in season. Very richly flavoured meat

stovies – a mash of mince beef, mixed with onions, spices and potatoes and then fired in meat dripping

white pudding – a white version of black pudding

PIES

bridie – Scottish version of English pasty; a hot pastry usually filled with meat

Kingdom of Fife pie – pie originating from across the Firth of Forth in Fife. Basically a rabbit pie with liver and pickled pork

Scotch pie – takeaway food, a stodgy pie consisting of lamb mince and spices, encased within pastry

stalker's pie – close to the English shepherd's pie, with venison being the main meat used

SNACKS

(the) chippie – Scots name for the local fast-food outlet. An amazingly diverse place that specialises in fried everything, but often also serves pizzas, kebabs, cigarettes, cold medicine, etc

chips wi' Broon sauce – a very Edinburgh phenomenon: fatty chips wrapped in newspapers smothered in the wondrous 'broon' sauce

Scotch eggs – whole shelled boiled eggs served inside a breadcrumb mix

toasties – toasted sandwiches served with a variety of fillings

SWEETS

butterscotch – a hard and brittle toffee made with butter and brown sugar

Edinburgh rock – chalkier version of the confectionery that is sold all over Scotland

VEGETABLES

clapshot – neeps and tatties mixed with spring onions, usually served as an accompaniment to haggis

colcannon – a Highland dish of carrot, turnip, cabbage and spices

kale – a leafy winter green used in a variety of dishes. Traditionally replaced by wild nettles in the summer

neeps – the Scots name for turnips, part of Scotland's national dish along with haggis

tatties – the Scots name for potatoes, also part of Scotland's national dish with haggis

Recipes

Haggis, neeps and tatties

Scotland's national dish is something that most people either love or hate. Those who love it will find that it is a surprisingly easy dish to prepare, given that few cooks ever attempt to make their own haggis. Purist cooks will have to accept pre-made haggis unless they fancy the prospect of disembowelling their own sheep and stealing the secret haggis recipe from Macsweens.

Haggis is easy to find on sale all over the city, as are the other ingredients in this recipe, which you can find in supermarkets and many of the shops featured in this book. If you happen to be in town on either Burns Night (26 January) or St

Andrew's Day (30 November), the entire country will seem to be eating haggis and you will have to join in. If you are back home on one of these big nights, instil fear amongst your friends by inviting them around for haggis, bring out the Macsweens and get cooking.

Serves three to four people.

Preparation time is around 30 minutes.

INGREDIENTS

Four Man Haggis
500g neeps (turnips/swedes)
500g tatties (potatoes)
A pinch of salt
A pinch of black pepper
One dram of single malt whisky per person
Two knobs of butter

Peel the neeps and tatties and boil in separate pots with a pinch of salt.

Boil some water and add the haggis. Cook according to the instructions on the packet, which varies depending on the exact type of haggis and the manufacturer.

Mash the neeps and tatties separately with the knobs of butter.

Slash open the haggis and serve, along with equal portions of the neeps and tatties. Add salt and black pepper to the neeps and tatties to taste.

Serve with a single dram of malt whisky.

Haggis gourmet style

If you want to create a more sophisticated dish, this idea comes from **Logie Baird's Bar** (*see page 13*), which serves its haggis, neeps and tatties with a whisky sauce.

To prepare the whisky sauce, heat a single dram of blended whisky (Logie Baird's suggests Teachers) together with double cream for five minutes.

Do not allow it to come to the boil and add a touch of coriander.

Either place this in a separate dish or drizzle it over the haggis.

For that real gourmet touch, copy many of the city's finer

▲ Haggis, neeps and tatties, with whisky sauce in side dishes